Succeed in English

Published by
Arcturus Publishing Limited
For Index Books Limited
Henson Way
Kettering
Northamptonshire
NN16 8PX

This edition published 2003

ISBN 1-84193-131-4

Printed and bound in China

Author: Hilary Sanders
Illustrator: Jim Hansen
Editor: Rebecca Panayiotou
Cover designer: Alex Ingr

Succeed in English

A simple and clear guide to understanding the principles of English grammar, punctuation and spelling.

Key Stage 2 Lower

Ages 7 to 9 years

Hilary Sanders

INDEX

Introduction

English grammar, punctuation and spelling can sometimes be daunting. Children take a while to grasp complicated rules only to find that there are often exceptions.

This book attempts to make the understanding of these rules of English as simple and clear as possible. The book is divided into three main sections: grammar, punctuation and spelling. Topics are clearly marked and explanations are thorough and clear.

By the end of Key Stage 2, children should have a good knowledge of the nature and use of verbs, nouns, adjectives, adverbs and pronouns. Punctuation should be at a high level and children should have at their fingertips a knowledge of where to place capital letters, commas, question marks and full stops. They should be familiar with the apostrophe and how to write direct speech, and spelling should be accurate.

This book attempts to make the understanding of these rules of English as simple and clear as possible. The book is laid out so that parents can help their children read through and understand the principles and rules of a topic on one page, while on the opposite page are exercises to test the child's understanding of these. The book has been designed so that most of the answers can be written straight on to the page. However, there are occasions when your child will need a working notebook.

Your child can work through this book at his/her own speed. A topic a day can be covered, or more if the child has the energy.

Each time your child has completed a page of this book, give them lots of praise and encouragement. Increase their sense of achievement by awarding them a star.

Within a short period of time you should find that your child's understanding will improve and he/she will approach English with greater confidence and accuracy.

Good luck and good practising!

Contents

Sentences

A sentence is a group of words that makes sense. We all use sentences when we speak and when we write. A sentence can be ***a statement*, *a question or a command***. Here are some examples:

★ The boy ran home.	(A statement)
★ Did the boy run home?	(A question, needing an answer)
★ Run home now.	(A command)

Complete and incomplete sentences

A sentence should make **complete sense on its own.**

★ The dog chased the cat.	(Complete)
★ Dog chased	(Incomplete, doesn't make sense)

Beginning a sentence

A sentence always **begins** with a **capital letter**.

★ **Y**esterday I walked to school.
★ **W**ho said that?

Ending a sentence

A sentence **ends** with a **full stop** or an **exclamation mark** if it is a statement.

★ These are your tickets**.**
★ Peter came first**!**

(Exclamation marks are used to show excitement or feeling. The exclamation mark shows that you need to read the sentence with expression.)

When a sentence is a question, it ends with a **question mark**.

★ Who did that**?**

Test 1

Now try these:

Put a tick next to each complete sentence:

1. David scored a hat trick. ☐
2. brave teacher ☐
3. Please can you help me? ☐
4. fast jump ☐
5. horse neigh ☐
6. You have won a prize! ☐
7. Where is my case? ☐
8. They were clever. ☐
9. fluffy cat ☐
10. "Ouch!" cried the boy. ☐

The computer has forgotten to punctuate these sentences. Can you correct them? The first one has been done for you.

11. at last, the postman came — At last, the postman came.
12. the car had been stolen — the car had been stolen
13. i had fish and chips for tea — I had fish and chips
14. adam wanted a football ______
15. how did you mend the fence ______
16. i have won the lottery ______
17. when did you arrive ______
18. it was cold at the seaside ______
19. stanley began to sing ______
20. where shall I meet you ______

Nouns

A noun tells us what someone or something is called. A noun can be the name of a living thing, an object, a place or an emotion. Here are some examples:

Living things	Objects	Places	Emotions
dog, cat, plant, human, Sally, he, she, I, you, they	car, cup, chair, bed, book, aeroplane, bread	kitchen, park, London, field, America	love, jealousy, anger, trust, passion

Common nouns

All the things we can see, hear, touch, smell, taste or feel are common nouns.

For example:

★ The **sheep** bleated softly.
★ The **radio** played.
★ The **eggs** were cooking.

Some sentences have more than one noun:

★ The **postman** delivered the **letters**.
★ The **helicopter** flew above the **town**.
★ The old **lady**, the young **girl**, the **boy**, the **dog** and the **cat** ran after the **gingerbread man**.

Underline the common nouns in these sentences:

1. The <u>bird</u> sang sweetly.
2. The boy ran.
3. The mouse was grey.
4. The paint was wet.
5. The old man was sleeping.
6. The girl went to school.
7. The teacher wrote a report.
8. The woman walked into the room.

9. Read the words. Decide which ones are nouns and write them in the noun box.

boy	fish	cup	run	jump	bridge
river	read	book	eat	climb	clock
hop	rabbit	dress	sleep	toffee	bedroom

Noun Box

Use these nouns to complete the sentences:

book **jelly** **cake** **popstar**

10. When I grow up I want to be a ____________________ .

11. Which ____________________ should I read?

12. Would you like a ____________________ for your birthday or would you prefer a chocolate ____________________ ?

Proper and Collective Nouns

Proper nouns

Proper nouns are nouns that name a *particular* or *special* person, place or thing. Proper nouns always start with a **capital letter**.

So, **house** is a *common noun* referring to anyone's dwelling, but **Houses of Parliament** is a *proper noun* because it refers to a particular building.

Similarly, **fish** is a *common noun* as it can refer to any fish, but **Koi** is a *proper noun* referring to one type of fish.

Your name is a proper noun. Other examples of proper nouns are **the days of the week, the months of the year and place names.**

Sentences can contain both proper nouns and common nouns. For example:

- He plays *football* on **Saturday**.
- **London** is the capital *city* of **England**.
- **Mrs. Sanders** is my *teacher.*
- *Lambs* are born in the **Spring**.
- My favourite *author* is **Beatrix Potter**.
- Her *cat* is called **Bongo**.

Collective nouns

A collective noun is a noun that names a *group* of things, people or animals. For example:

- A **pack** of dogs
- A **pod** of dolphins
- A **class** of children
- A **nest** of vipers

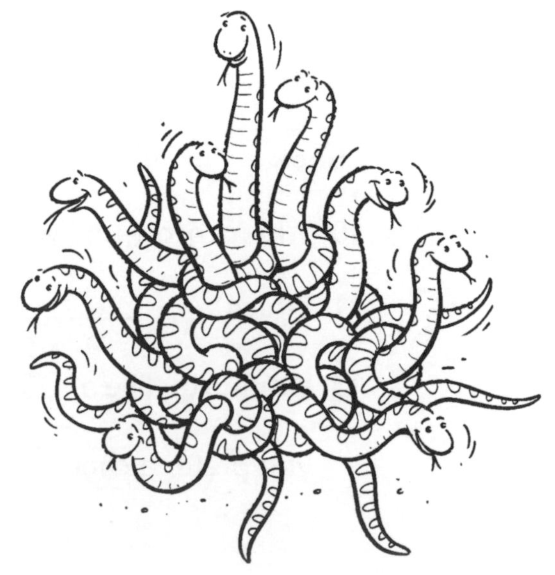

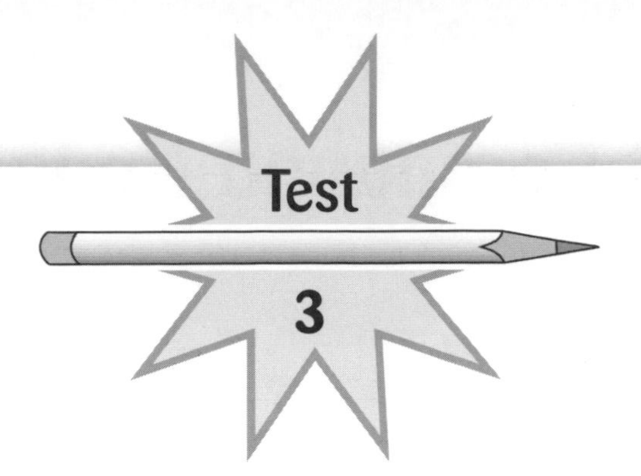

Read these sentences and list the nouns in the correct box.

1. Beckham plays football for Manchester United.
2. My birthday is in October.
3. Friday is five days after Sunday.
4. Queen Elizabeth II has opened a new bridge.
5. The class went to Paris through the Channel Tunnel.

Proper nouns	Common nouns

Choose the correct word to complete the sentence:

flock **pack** **class** **shoal** **swarm**

6. A ____________________ of dogs roamed the estate.
7. A ____________________ of sheep grazed in the field.
8. The ____________________ of fish raced away from the shark.
9. The ____________________ of children raised two hundred pounds.
10. The ____________________ of bees buzzed angrily.
11. A ____________________ of birds flew in the sky.

Abstract and Compound Nouns

Abstract nouns

An abstract noun is a noun that refers to an idea, state, emotion or a quality rather than an object.

For example, ***love*** is an abstract noun – it cannot be seen, touched or heard in the way that you can see, touch and hear a car, but you can see the way that love might cause someone to behave.

Here are some other examples of abstract nouns:

- ★ We are in **love**.
- ★ Mary had a clever **idea**.
- ★ The purpose of the law is to uphold **justice**.
- ★ I want to know the **truth**.
- ★ He had great **faith** in God.
- ★ The play was a great **success**.
- ★ Johnny was filled with **anger** and **hate**.
- ★ The people wanted **power** and **freedom**.
- ★ She was amazed at her friend's **generosity**.

Compound nouns

A compound noun is a word made up from two smaller words to form a new word with its own meaning.

For example:

- ★ **hand** and **bag** together become **handbag**
- ★ **light** and **house** together become **lighthouse**

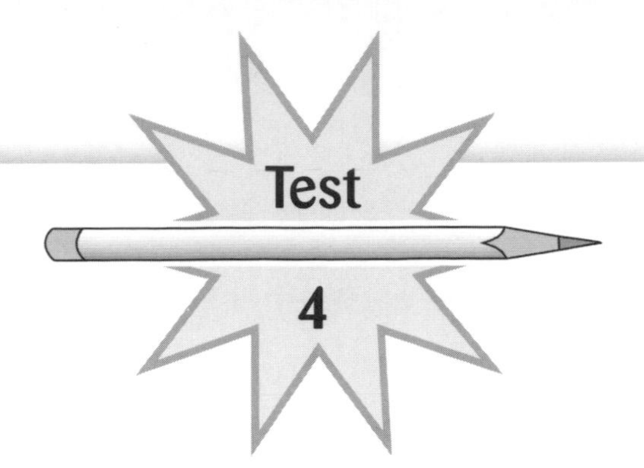

1. Write the abstract nouns on to the heart and the common nouns on to the table.

justice	door	banana	love	tree
van	envy	milk	football	faith
bin	resentment	truth	book	shoe
jealousy	fire	fear	hate	hope

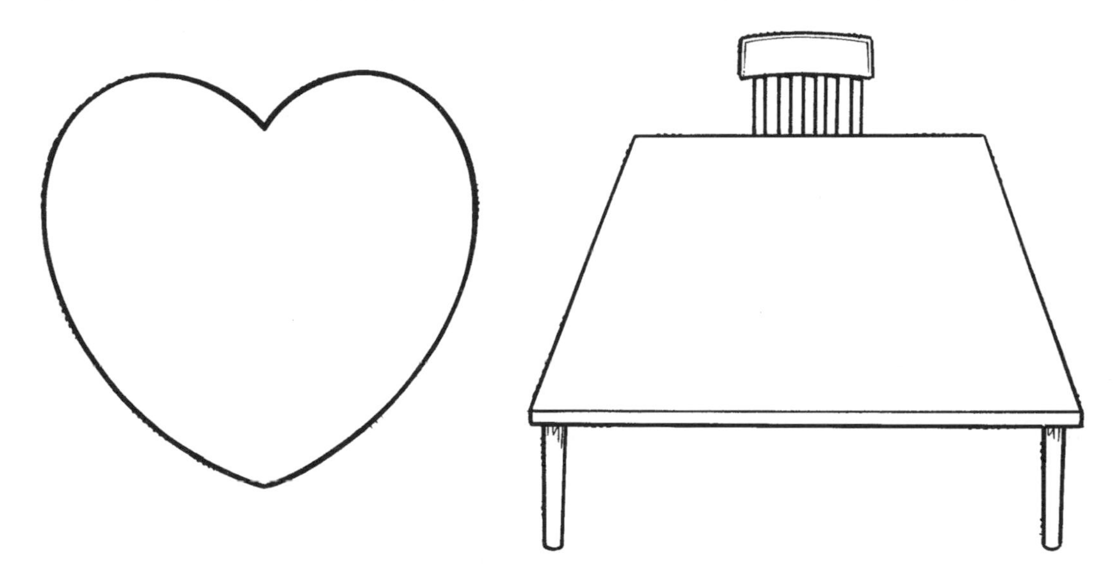

Read the sentences. Decide which word is a compound noun and underline it. Write the two words from which it is formed in the spaces provided. The first one has been done for you.

2. Sarah sat on the armchair. arm + chair

3. The postman delivered the letter. ________ + ________

4. Dad makes tea in the teapot. ________ + ________

5. Gabriella chose a red toothbrush. ________ + ________

6. The baby sat in her playpen. ________ + ________

Pronouns

Pronouns are the names we call each other when we are not using our "proper" names. Here are some examples:

I, you, he, she, it, we, they, his, hers.

Pronouns are often used to avoid repeating a noun that has already been mentioned. For example, look at the sentences below:

Cinderella is a good girl. All day long Cinderella works and works in the house. Cinderella's two sisters are very lazy and don't help Cinderella one bit. Cinderella's sisters are happy because Cinderella's sisters are going to a ball. Cinderella's sisters will see the prince. Cinderella can't go to the ball. Cinderella has no ball dress or shoes. Instead, Cinderella will have to work in Cinderella's stepmother's house. Cinderella is very unhappy. Cinderella also wants to go to the ball and see the prince.

Quite long and clumsy – don't you agree? We can rewrite it much more neatly like this:

Cinderella is a good girl. All day long **she** works and works in the house. **Her** two sisters are very lazy and don't help **her** one bit. **They** are happy because **they** are going to a ball. **They** will see the prince. Cinderella can't go to the ball. **She** has no ball dress or shoes. Instead, **she** will have to work in **her** stepmother's house. **She** is very unhappy. **She** also wants to go to the ball and see the prince.

You can see from these passages how useful pronouns are! Rather than repeating the words ***Cinderella*** and ***Cinderella's sisters*** over and over again, we can use a pronoun in their place. When we are chatting to our friends, we do this all the time without even thinking about it!

Personal pronouns

Personal pronouns refer to people and things.

★ **He** is a teacher.
★ Sue and Helen are going to the park. **They** will play on the swings.
★ This book is interesting. **It** is about dinosaurs.

Possessive pronouns

Possessive pronouns show who something belongs to.

★ **Her** hair is dark brown; **his** hair is blonde.
★ **Our** holiday was great, but **theirs** was a disaster.

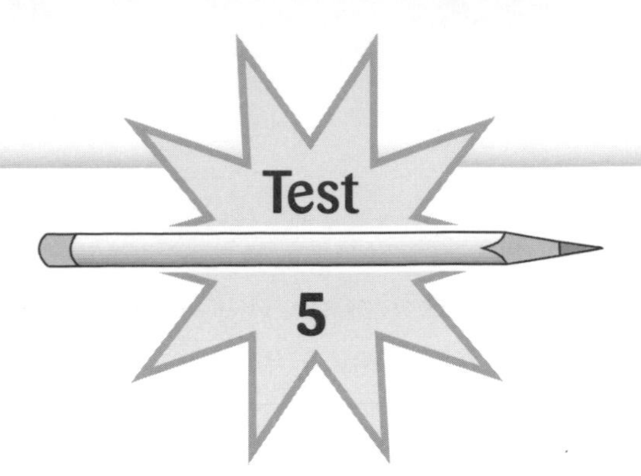

1. Here is a table showing personal and possessive pronouns. Can you write your own sentence using each of the pronouns? You may need to write your examples on a separate sheet of paper. The first one has been done for you.

PRONOUNS – PERSONAL AND POSSESSIVE

	Singular	Plural	Singular Possessive	Plural Possessive
1st person	I I ran to catch the bus.	we ______ ______	mine ______ ______	ours ______ ______
2nd person	you ______ ______	you ______ ______	yours ______ ______	yours ______ ______
3rd person	he/she/it ______ ______	they ______ ______	his/hers/its ______ ______	theirs ______ ______

2. You will need a separate sheet of paper for this exercise. Read the story. Now try to rewrite it, replacing the underlined words with the correct pronoun. Remember to read your sentences to make sure that they make sense.

The boy stared at the monster. The monster stared back at the boy. Suddenly, the boy turned and ran as fast as the boy could. Screeching at the top of the monster's voice, the monster gave chase. Closer and closer the monster came until, with a mighty leap, the monster seized the boy. The boy gave a loud scream and the monster dropped the boy. The boy ran home to the boy's mother. The boy's mother cuddled the boy and then the mother phoned the police.

Verbs

A verb is the action word in a sentence. It is a part of speech that tells you what a person or thing does and how they are.

A sentence needs a verb. In a sentence, a verb can tell us:

How we move	e.g.	run, walk, tiptoe
How we talk	e.g.	whisper, shout, giggle
How we feel	e.g.	love, hate, like

There are thousands of actions we take part in, feel or talk about every day!

In a sentence, the verb tells us **what is happening.** For example:

★ Steve **jumped** over the fence.

In this example, the verb is **"jumped"** and it tells us what Steve did.

Verb chain

Now look at this sentence:

★ Steve **was sleeping** in his bed.

In this example, **two words** tell us what Steve is doing – **was sleeping**. When there are two words that tell us what is happening in a sentence, we call them a **verb chain**.

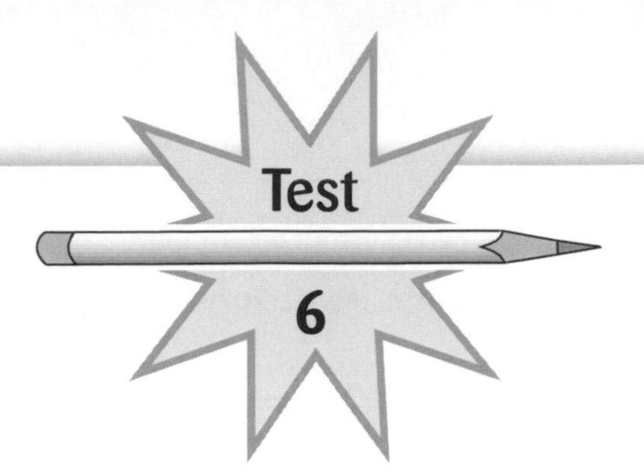

Read these sentences and write the verb or verb chain in the box.

1. Tessa cooks dinner.

2. He walked to the station.

3. I am writing a story.

4. The boy will run the marathon.

5. Blake waited for Emily.

6. Carol was drinking her tea.

7. David buys a magazine.

8. Meena loves Arsenal.

9. Mum wants dessert.

10. I am telephoning my friend.

Choose the appropriate verb to complete the sentences below.

laughs **writes** **rides** **cries**

11. The children ________________ comics.

12. John ________________ his bike after school.

13. The baby ________________ for her mummy.

14. The audience ________________ at the comedian.

15. Sally ________________ a letter.

Verb Tenses

The tense of a verb tells you when its action takes place – in the present, the past, or the future.

Present tense

The present tense tells you what is happening now.

★ I **am** laughing.
★ He **is** working.

Future tense

The future tense tells you about what will happen in the future.

★ Tomorrow **will be** my birthday.
★ I **will do** the washing up after dinner.

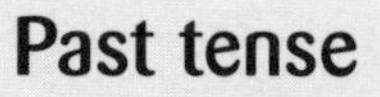

Past tense

The past tense tells you about what has happened in the past.

★ I **was** happy yesterday.
★ Annie **did** a lot of work.

VERB TENSES – TO BE

Present	Past	Future
I am	I was	I will be
You are	You were	You will be
He is	He was	He will be
She is	She was	She will be
It is	It was	It will be
We are	We were	We will be
You are (pl.)	You were (pl.)	You will be (pl.)
They are	They were	They will be

VERB TENSES – TO HAVE

Present	Past	Future
I have	I had	I will have
You have	You had	You will have
He has	He had	He will have
She has	She had	She will have
It has	It had	It will have
We have	We had	We will have
You have (pl.)	You had (pl.)	You will have (pl.)
They have	They had	They will have

Underline the verbs or verb chains in these sentences and write the verb's tense in the box. The first one has been done for you.

1. Kieren skips to school.	present
2. Tommy wanted an icecream.	
3. We will enter the competition.	
4. I passed the exam!	
5. They love this cake.	
6. I am intelligent.	
7. The dog will chew the sofa.	
8. John polished his shoes.	
9. You will enjoy this film.	

Use the tables on the previous page to help you write the correct form of the verb "to be" or "to have" in these sentences. Remember to read them back to yourself to check that they make sense.

10. Last night, you ____had____ salt and vinegar on your chips.

11. Tomorrow, I ______________ make a cake.

12. They ______________ smile when I tell them the good news.

13. Before we left the shop, we ______________ asked to choose a free gift.

14. I ______________ get up early tomorrow morning.

15. We ______________ a great time when we went to Greece last year.

16. She ______________ very happy at the moment.

Use of the Tenses in Writing

When writing a set of instructions or a non-chronological report (one that is not linked to time), the present tense is used.

For **instruction writing** this is because the instructions will be followed in the present and are like a set of orders. For example, look at these instructions for finding the answers to the tests in this book:

1. **Find** the test number at the top of the test you have completed.
2. **Turn** to the back of the book, **keeping** your finger in the test page.
3. **Find** the number of the test in the answer section.
4. **Compare** your answer with the one that is given.

In the case of **non-chronological reports**, the report is usually about something that still exists, for example, frogs, and so is written in the present tense. For example:

Frogs
Frogs **are** amphibians. They **live** in and near ponds and lakes. After mating, the female **lays** her spawn in the pond. The frog spawn **hatches** into tadpoles. The tadpoles **change** and **grow** into frogs. The frog's life cycle **is** an example of metamorphosis.

Types of writing that use the future tense include newspaper articles advertising shows and events that have not yet been held, and predictions of things that may happen or change in the future. For example, look at the following newspaper article describing a bonfire party to take place in the future:

Sparkle in the Dark
On November 5 there **will be** a bonfire party at the park. The event, called "Sparkle in the Dark", **will be** the largest display of fireworks in the South East. Pyrotechnic experts **will launch** at least 200 rockets into the air in 15 minutes.

As you can see, many future tense verbs are **verb chains**, using **will** plus another verb.

Choose the correct verb to complete the instructions below on making an omelette.

crack	heat	sprinkle
add	pour	turn
cook	whisk	serve

1. First ________________ two eggs into a bowl.
2. ________________ a small amount of milk.
3. ________________ some salt and pepper into the mixture.
4. ________________ the mixture with a fork.
5. ________________ some oil in a frying pan.
6. ________________ the egg mixture into the pan.
7. ________________ for a few minutes.
8. ________________ the omelette over and cook for another minute.
9. ________________ with toast.

10. Change this report of an event from the past tense into the future tense. Write the new report on to a separate sheet of paper. The words you need to change have been underlined. As well as changing the tense, sometimes you might need to add a word to make the sentence make sense.

Last week, there was a fete at the school. There were many stalls. The cake stall was popular and sold a wide range of cakes and sweets. The raffle raised at least £200 for the school. The fete was opened by the mayor, and she gave a donation to the school on behalf of the council. The fete began at 2 o'clock and finished at 4 o'clock. The school were delighted as enough money was raised to buy four new computers.

Simple and Compound Sentences

Simple sentence

A simple sentence consists of a single clause.
A clause is a part of a sentence that contains a subject and a verb.

For example:

* The *ballerina* **danced** all night.
* *Annie* **watched** the television.

Compound sentence

A compound sentence consists of two main clauses joined together by a word like **and**, **but**, or **or**.
A main clause is one that makes sense on its own.

For example:

a) Joe likes chocolate drops **and** he likes toffee.

b) Peter was late **but** Chris waited.
c) I can walk home **or** I can catch the bus.

Each clause in these sentences makes sense on its own.

When the subject and the verb of the second clause in the sentence are the same as the subject and the verb in the first, the sentence can be shortened and it will still make sense.

So:

a) Could become: Joe likes chocolate drops and toffee.
b) Cannot be changed. (**Peter** is the subject of the first clause, **Chris** is the subject of the second clause.)
c) Could become: I can walk home or catch the bus.

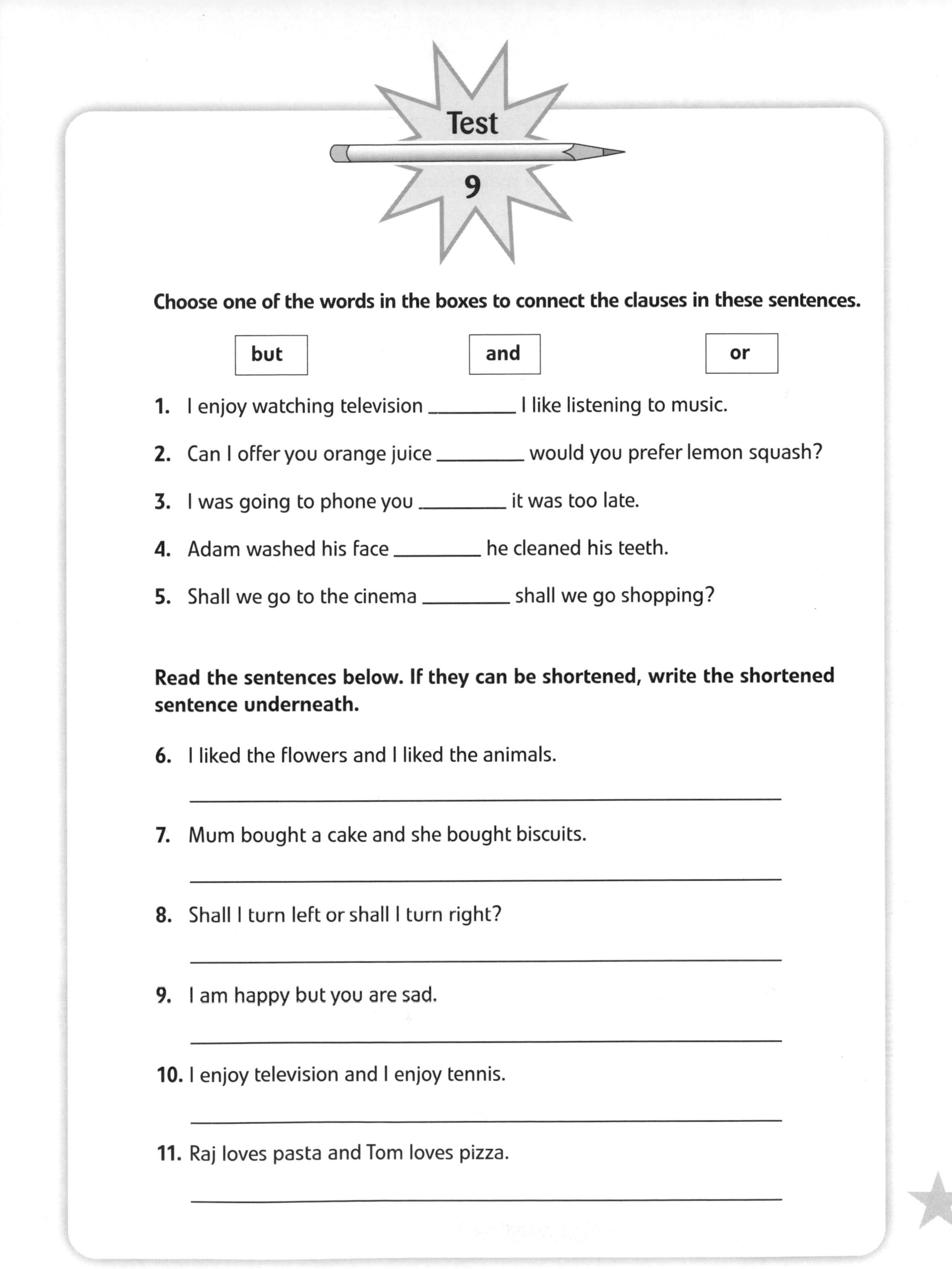

Test 9

Choose one of the words in the boxes to connect the clauses in these sentences.

but	and	or

1. I enjoy watching television ________ I like listening to music.
2. Can I offer you orange juice ________ would you prefer lemon squash?
3. I was going to phone you ________ it was too late.
4. Adam washed his face ________ he cleaned his teeth.
5. Shall we go to the cinema ________ shall we go shopping?

Read the sentences below. If they can be shortened, write the shortened sentence underneath.

6. I liked the flowers and I liked the animals.

   ____

7. Mum bought a cake and she bought biscuits.

   ____

8. Shall I turn left or shall I turn right?

   ____

9. I am happy but you are sad.

   ____

10. I enjoy television and I enjoy tennis.

   ____

11. Raj loves pasta and Tom loves pizza.

   ____

Complex Sentences

A complex sentence consists of a main clause and a subordinate clause.

Within a complex sentence, one clause will make **complete sense on its own**, and is called the **main clause.**

The other clause will **not make complete sense** if separated from the main clause and read on its own. This clause is called the **subordinate clause**.

A subordinate clause gives additional information about the main clause. It begins with a conjunction like ***when***, ***because***, ***if*** or ***although***.

For example:

★ **Beverley went for a walk**, although it was raining.

MAIN CLAUSE
– makes sense on its own

SUBORDINATE CLAUSE
– does not make sense on its own

Sometimes the subordinate clause can be put at the **beginning** or in the **middle** of the sentence and the sentence will still make sense.

For example:

★ Although it was raining, **Beverley went for a walk**.
★ **Beverley**, although it was raining, **went for a walk**.

Read the sentences and underline the main clause. (Remember: the main clause can be read on its own and will make sense.)

1. April was excited because she had won the raffle.
2. Although it was a sunny day, Bill wore his coat.
3. Robyn, laughing softly, crept out of the room.
4. Because he dropped his ice cream, Jake cried.
5. The dog, wagging its tail, ran towards the cat.
6. After spitting at the dog, the cat turned and jumped on to the fence.

Use these conjunctions to link the clauses to make complex sentences.

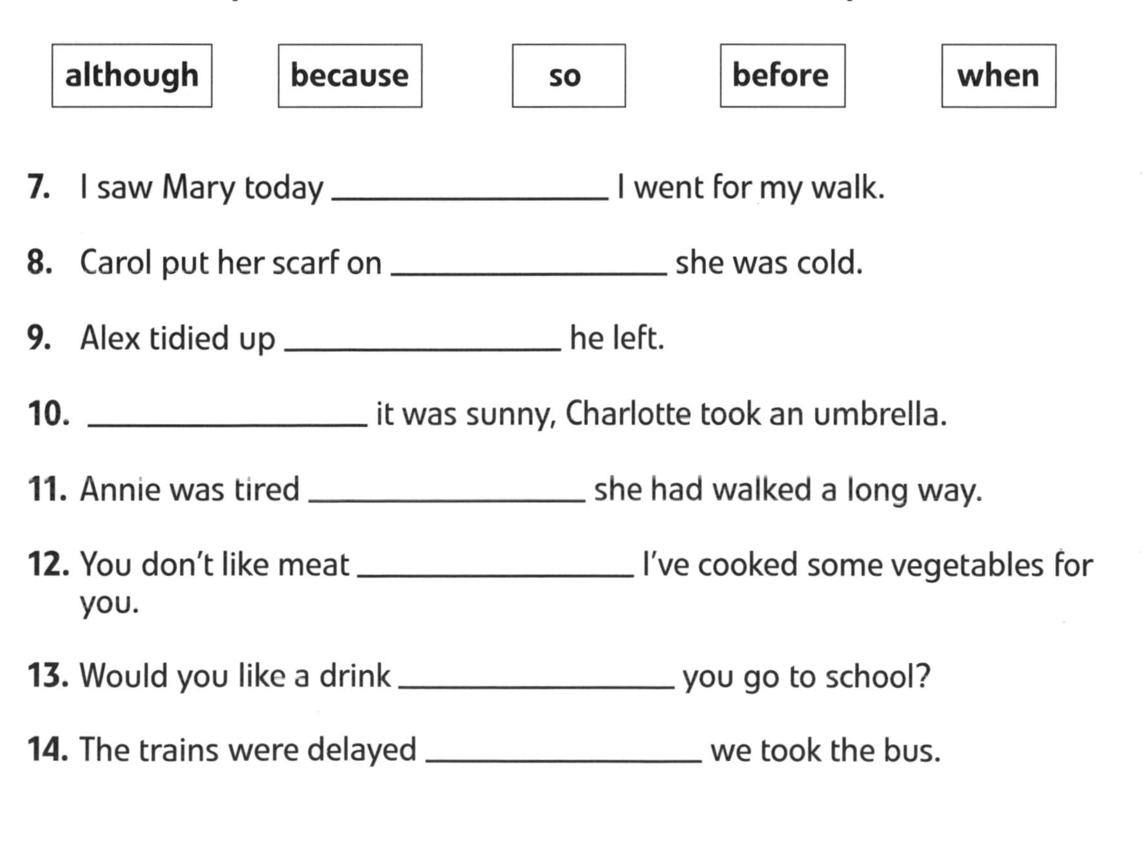

although	**because**	**so**	**before**	**when**

7. I saw Mary today ______________ I went for my walk.
8. Carol put her scarf on ______________ she was cold.
9. Alex tidied up ______________ he left.
10. ______________ it was sunny, Charlotte took an umbrella.
11. Annie was tired ______________ she had walked a long way.
12. You don't like meat ______________ I've cooked some vegetables for you.
13. Would you like a drink ______________ you go to school?
14. The trains were delayed ______________ we took the bus.

Adjectives

As you have learned, nouns are words that name objects, living things, and concepts.

For example:

★ The **chair** was beside the desk.

In this sentence, **chair** is a noun (and so is **desk**). However, when you read the sentence you could imagine any kind of chair: a dining chair, a small chair, a plastic chair, a blue chair, a barber's chair, and so on. To give a more **precise description** of the chair, an **adjective** is needed.

Adjectives are used to give more information about the noun in a sentence, i.e. they add more detail.

So, the sentence could be rewritten to include an adjective:

★ The **swivel** chair was beside the desk.
★ The **orange** chair was beside the desk.
★ The **huge**, **metal** chair was beside the desk.

Adjectives can be used to create atmosphere in settings and to show the personality of characters.

For example:

★ "When are you coming home?" asked her **furious** father.
★ "I am the richest man in the world," boasted the **arrogant** tycoon.
★ Jamila was a **modest** child.
★ The **dark** night swirled around the **gloomy** castle.
★ The **gentle** sea stroked the **smooth**, **sandy** beach.

Write down the adjectives in these sentences.

1. The hot sun shone down. ____________________

2. The fierce knight charged. ____________________

3. A strong wind blew the leaves away. ____________________

4. Sitting on a grey stone, there was an elf. ____________________

5. The miserable girl wailed. ____________________

6. I told a funny joke. ____________________

7. Mary had a small kitten. ____________________

8. The children ate the delicious chocolates. ____________________

9. The beautiful swan glided across the river. ____________________

10. The happy dog ran up the path. ____________________

Choose the adjective that is opposite in meaning to the one already used in these sentences and write it on the line.

bold	furious	boastful	wise	mean	tiny

11. The **calm** man stared at the window. ____________________

12. The **foolish** woman offered advice to the group. ____________________

13. The **shy** child sat in the front row. ____________________

14. The **modest** student won first prize. ____________________

15. Hannah ate a **huge** slice of cake. ____________________

16. The **generous** boy shared his sweets. ____________________

Adjectives 2

The adjectives in the previous exercise were all placed next to the noun in the sentence. But sometimes **the adjective may be separated from the noun by one or more words**.

For example:

- ★ The **handsome** man waved.
- ★ The man, who waved, was **handsome**.

In both of these sentences, **handsome** is the adjective because it **gives us more information** about the man. The fact that the position of the adjective in the sentence has changed is not important.

Choosing adjectives

There are many adjectives that have similar meanings and to make your writing interesting and precise it is important to choose an adjective that best fits the noun and the sentence.

For example:

The **bright** sunlight shone down on the **bright** flowers. Charley, who was wearing her **bright** top, skipped through the meadow towards the **bright** water.

Reading these two sentences is boring because the adjective **bright** has been overused. To make the passage more interesting, we need to change some of the "brights" to another adjective with a similar, more precise meaning. Using a **thesaurus** will help us to find a list of other words to use instead. The sentences could then be changed to read:

The **brilliant** sunlight shone down on the **vivid**, **colourful** flowers. Charley, who was wearing her **bright red** top, skipped through the meadow towards the **dazzling** water.

This makes the passage far more interesting as we have painted a more imaginative, detailed picture through our choice of words.

The adjectives in the large sack have been jumbled up. They are adjectives that could be used to describe: feeling happy or sad, brave or cowardly. Can you sort the words into the correct sack? Look them up if you're not sure what they mean.

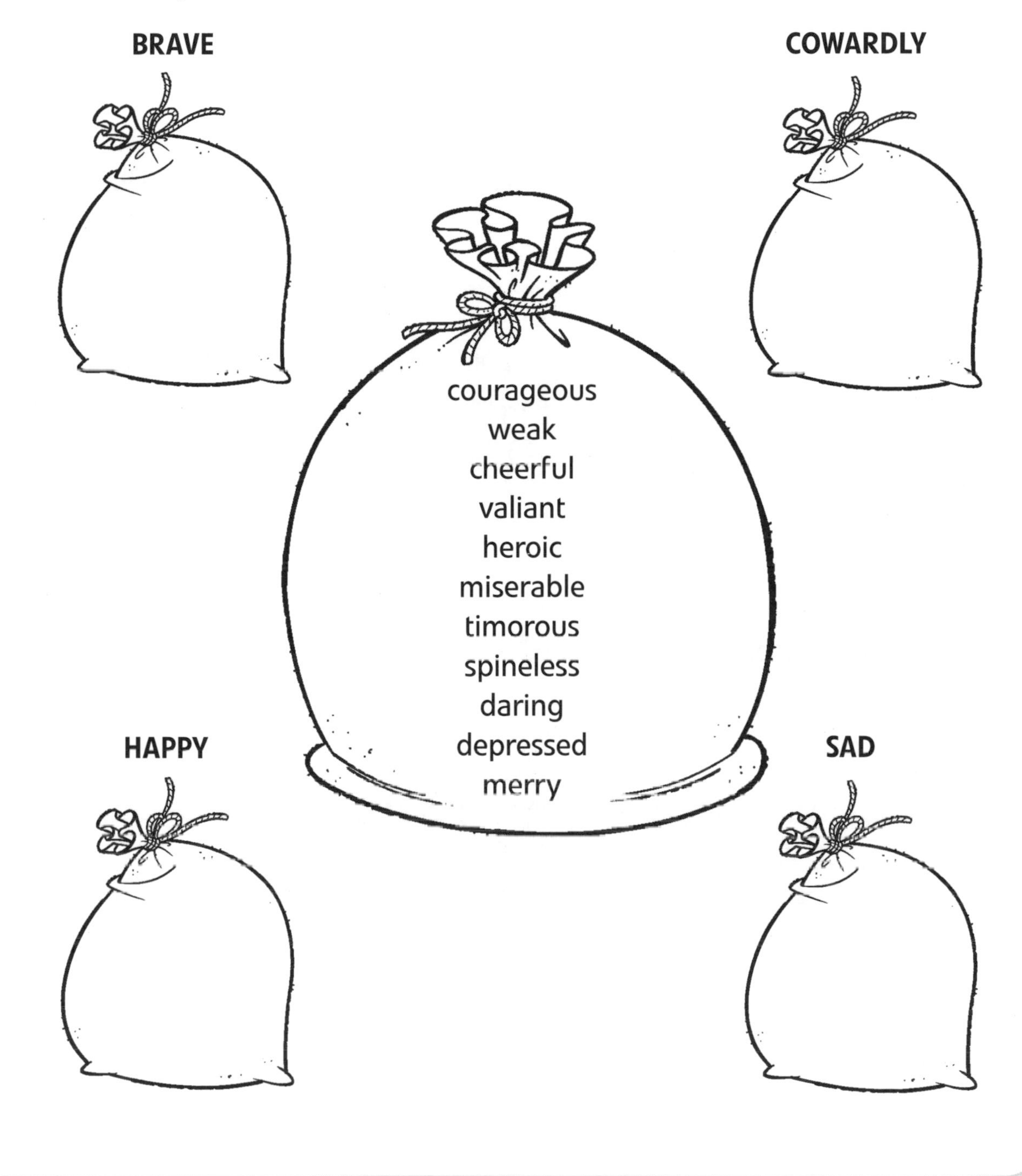

Determiners

Determiners are words that make it clear which particular thing we are referring to.

Examples of determiners are:

this, that, these, those, the, each, every, my, your, her, his, its, our, their

As you can see, many determiners are pronouns. Using the correct determiner is important when writing about more than one of something. For example, imagine you are writing a story about two children taking their dogs for a walk in the park. It would be confusing and difficult to know which dog was being referred to in the story if only "the" was used, as seen here:

A boy and a girl took their dogs for a walk. The dog jumped in the lake. The dog stayed dry. The dog shook itself and splashed water everywhere. The girl gave the dog a pat and took it home.

Using more specific determiners makes the story clearer:

A boy and a girl took their dogs for a walk. **His** dog jumped in the lake. **Her** dog stayed dry. **His** dog shook itself and splashed water everywhere. The girl gave **her** dog a pat and took it home.

	1st person		2nd person		3rd person	
	s	**pl**	**s**	**pl**	**s**	**pl**
Pronoun	I	we	you	you	he, she, it,	they
Determiner	my	our	your	your	his, her, its,	their

Underline the determiners in these sentences. The first one has been done for you.

1. These trainers belong to David.
2. Her hair is beautiful.
3. Every child was given a present.
4. Their basket was full.
5. Our fruit is ripe but your fruit is not.
6. My car is red; that car is silver.
7. This Saturday it is our birthday.
8. Each Sunday we go to the gym.
9. Those children are very noisy.
10. That cat lives in the town but this cat lives on the boat.

Read the sentences and write the correct determiners in the spaces.

his	her	their	my	our	its	your

11. He searched for ________ football. (3rd person singular)
12. They asked for ________ tea. (3rd person plural)
13. I would like to go to ________ house. (1st person singular)
14. Well done, you have found ________ letter. (2nd person singular)
15. We performed well in ________ school play. (1st person plural)
16. It has lost ________ way. (3rd person singular)
17. Would you all like ________ dinner now? (2nd person plural)
18. They are worried about ________ sick cat. (3rd person plural)
19. Sophie loves ________ reflection in the mirror. (3rd person singular)
20. I have changed into ________ new trainers. (1st person singular)

Adverbs

An adverb is a part of speech that tells you more about a verb. An adverb tells you where, how, why, or how much something happens or is done.

For example:

- ★ Mary worked **quickly**.
- ★ Miranda sang **loudly**.
- ★ Raphael **usually** eats breakfast.
- ★ The dog **often** chews the sofa.

Adverbs are an important word class because they give extra meaning to verbs, making writing exciting and interesting to the reader. Look at the sentences below. In each sentence the only word that has changed is the adverb. Think about the picture that comes into your mind as you read each sentence.

- ★ Emily walked **confidently** across the room.
- ★ Emily walked **swiftly** across the room.
- ★ Emily walked **hesitantly** across the room.
- ★ Emily walked **slowly** across the room.
- ★ Emily walked **moodily** across the room.
- ★ Emily walked **cheerfully** across the room.

Each of these sentences now gives us quite a different picture. The adverbs tell us more about the verb "walked". They tell us ***how*** Emily walked.

Pick out the verbs in these sentences and underline them. Then write the adverbs in the space provided. The first one has been done for you.

1. She lovingly <u>stroked</u> his hand. lovingly

2. Joanna quickly ran up the stairs.

3. The man walked unsteadily.

4. The lady moved gracefully.

5. Sam painted beautifully.

6. Read this passage. Underline the adverbs in each sentence. Remember: don't confuse your adverbs with your adjectives!

Alice stopped abruptly and listened carefully. She could hear a groaning sound coming from the house. She walked slowly up the narrow garden path, stopping occasionally to listen for the noise. She hammered loudly on the door, but there was no answer. She took a deep breath and pushed firmly. The door swung open. She went in. With each step she took, the floorboards creaked loudly. Then the door of the bathroom opened and her father came out singing. The groaning noise was her father's awful singing!

Write in an adverb to show how each verb happened.

7. Amy ran ________________ down the road.

8. The dog growled ________________ .

9. ________________ , they sang the lullaby.

10. The boy walked ________________ through the woods.

Grammar Revision

In this section you will revise your knowledge of grammar. Let's see how much you remember. Good luck!

Sentences

For this section you will need to remember everything you have been learning about sentences.

Remember that a sentence must make complete sense. Can you group the following into the correct boxes?

1. my cat

2. How old are you?

3. My granny is quite old now.

4. Catherine

5. gave me a clock

6. The man travelled to work.

7. like

8. I need your help.

9. dog bark

10. My slippers are cosy.

Sentences	**Not sentences**

Which of these sentences are simple and which are compound? Write simple or compound in the box.

11. Jane did not like going to the dentist.

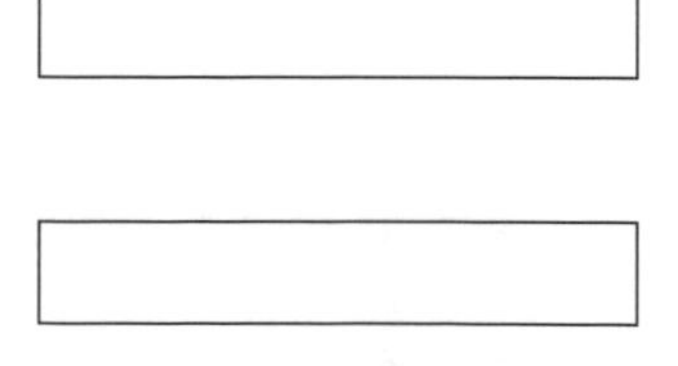

12. The dog is fond of his toy bone and he also likes to play with his ball.

13. Peter was nine years old.

14. Some people think that it is cruel to keep animals in zoos but other people would disagree.

15. You can drink tea or you can have some coffee.

16. Which words should you look out for when identifying a compound sentence? (There are three.)

________________ ________________ ________________

Complex sentences have a main and a subordinate clause. Don't forget that sometimes the main clause is separated by the subordinate clause.

Can you underline the subordinate clause in each of these sentences?

17. Whatever the weather, I enjoy walking.

18. Although the news is normally on late at night, I always stay up to watch it.

19. The girl couldn't go to school because she felt so unwell.

20. After trying so hard, Paul was disappointed that he didn't win the race.

21. Karen, chuckling softly to herself, hid under the blanket.

22. The man, who had been watching TV for a while, had fallen asleep.

23. These complex sentences have become muddled. Can you match each main clause with the correct subordinate clause? Join them with a line.

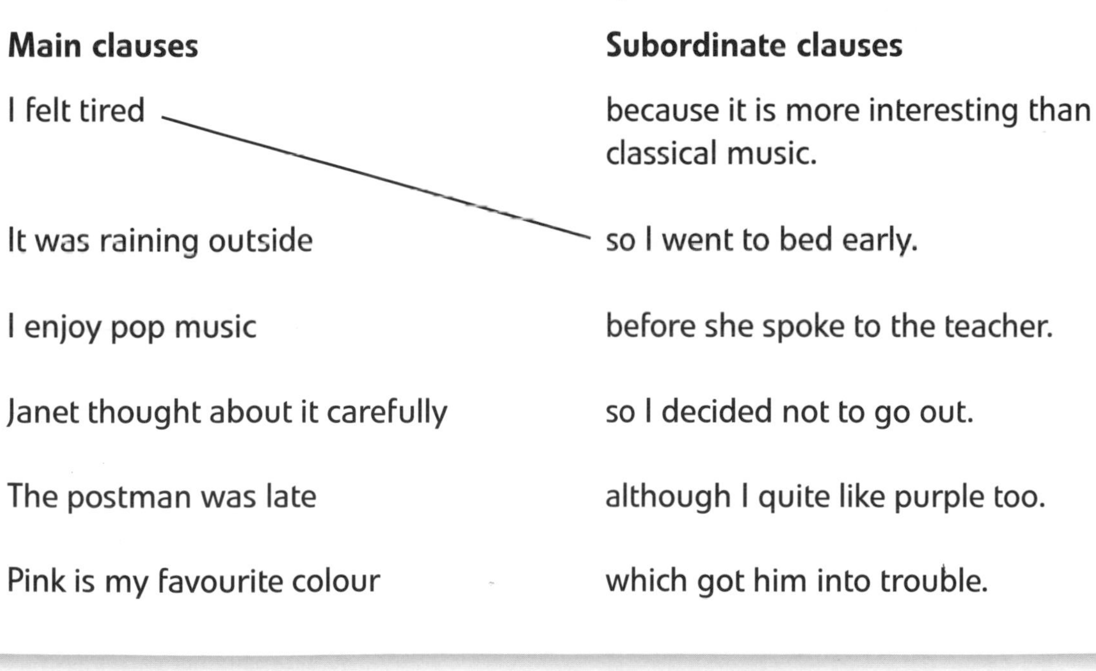

Grammar Revision

Nouns

For this section you will need to remember everything you have learnt about nouns.

Tick the words that are nouns:

1. radio ☐
2. feel ☐
3. village ☐
4. hatred ☐
5. slipper ☐
6. metal ☐
7. want ☐
8. tea ☐
9. pull ☐
10. money ☐

Most of the above nouns are common but which of these nouns are abstract? Tick the ones that refer to an idea, state or emotion.

11. anger ☐
12. honesty ☐
13. blackboard ☐
14. house ☐
15. rage ☐
16. pencil ☐

17. What is a proper noun? Write your answer below.

____

____

____

____

18. How is the way we write proper nouns different from the way we write common nouns? Write your answer below.

____

____

____

____

Now look at these sentences and identify the proper nouns by circling them and the common nouns by underlining them.

19. Charlie the clown wore striped trousers and a red nose.

20. The river Medway runs through Rochester.

21. Oranges and apples are juicy fruit.

22. Caroline was a teacher.

23. My sister's birthday is in June.

Some of the words in these sentences need capital letters because they are proper nouns. Can you correct them?

24. paris is the capital of france. ______________

25. I don't get on with george. ______________

26. On tuesday we always have P.E. ______________

27. My favourite character is harry potter. ______________

28. The tower of london is a fascinating tourist site. ______________

Grammar Revision

Can you put the correct collective noun into each of the sentences below? You might need a dictionary to help you.

gaggle	pack	audience	flight	family

29. A _________________ of hounds chased the fox.

30. A _________________ of geese ran towards the lake.

31. The _________________ enjoyed the performance.

32. I climbed the _________________ of stairs.

33. My _________________ is made up of my mum, my dad and my brother.

34. Write at least five different compound nouns in the box. Remember, you make them by combining two nouns.

book **worm** **case**

house **keeper**

boat **wife** **goal**

Compound nouns

Pronouns

You will remember that pronouns are used to replace proper nouns. Can you replace the repeated, underlined noun with an appropriate pronoun? Rewrite the new sentence underneath.

1. Mr Walker is my science teacher and Mr Walker also teaches mathematics.

____

____

2. The book was called "Succeed in English". The book helped me to improve my writing.

____

____

3. My family came to visit me. My family enjoyed themselves very much.

____

4. Catherine was a young girl and Catherine had long, straight hair.

____

Can you fill in the gaps with the correct possessive pronoun?

5. I've finished my homework and you haven't even started __________ yet.

6. That pencil case is not __________ . It's __________ !

7. The dog shook __________ tail.

8. The couple claimed that the cat was __________ .

Grammar Revision

Verbs

Now you need to think back to what you have learnt about verbs.

Can you circle the verbs or verb chains in these sentences? Some sentences may contain more than one verb.

1. You walk to school.

2. Stephen slept all afternoon.

3. Jodie wanted to visit her aunt.

4. I am going out now!

5. We were thinking about the film.

6. The bus stopped.

7. My mum went to the gym.

8. John drove back from his mum's house.

9. When I came home, the cat was clawing at the door.

10. Can you tell me the time?

Can you change these sentences so that each verb is in the past tense? Write your sentences underneath.

11. I enjoy the film last night.

____

12. Yesterday, the children play outside all day.

____

13. Before he went to the interview, James polish his shoes.

____

14. I ask you not to do that!

____

15. I go to the youth club.

____

16. Can you group these verbs and verb chains to show whether they are present, past or future forms of the verb?

will have	**has**	**went**	**go**	**will be**
was	**is**	**were**	**are**	**had**
talked	**did**	**wanted**	**make**	**made**

Past	Present	Future

17. Now choose one verb or verb chain from each box and write a sentence using it.

a. ____

____

b. ____

____

c. ____

____

Grammar Revision

18. It is important to be consistent in the use of tenses. Read the following text, in which the author keeps switching between the past and present tense. Can you rewrite the sentences, altering the underlined words so that the whole passage is in the past tense?

During the Victorian era children <u>are employed</u> to do a variety of unpleasant jobs. One of the worst jobs <u>is</u> working in a cotton mill. The children <u>have</u> to work incredibly hard. They crawled under heavy machinery and <u>risk</u> their lives every day. In addition, they <u>are</u> not paid very much and <u>live</u> in cramped, squalid conditions. Most children who worked in cotton mills <u>are</u> orphans, so they <u>do</u> not even have a family's love and support. Do you think you would have <u>enjoy</u> working in a cotton mill?

19. Why do you think this text should be written in the past tense?

20. Which tense are instructions normally written in and can you explain why?

21. When would you use the future tense?

Adverbs

In this section you will need to remember the different types of adverbs that you might use in your writing.

Underline the adverb that tells us **how** something happened.

1. John ate his apple slowly.

2. Carefully, the snooker player took aim.

3. Ralph stroked the cat gently.

4. Simon swung the bat fiercely.

5. Cheerfully, Father Christmas climbed down the chimney.

6. The wind was blowing furiously.

7. Jamie completed his homework quickly.

8. Fred kicked ruthlessly.

9. Manchester United plays fantastically.

10. Carolyn stomped around grumpily.

Underline the adverb that tells us **when or how often** something happened.

11. Occasionally, I eat chocolate.

12. I rarely go to the gym.

13. You can usually find me at youth club on Thursday.

14. Come here now!

15. You can come and visit me soon.

Grammar Revision

16. Read the following passage and insert the adverbs in the correct spaces.

often	downstairs	outside
dreamily	sometimes	inside

Jane stood ________________ Becky's house and wondered if her friend would answer the door. She was sure that Becky was ________________ because she could hear music coming from the lounge. She was probably gazing ________________ at her David Beckham poster, Jane concluded. This ________________ happened. Just as she was about to give up and go home, she caught sight of a figure tramping ________________ .
" ________________ ," thought Jane, "you make me so cross!"

Use these adverbs to write your own sentences. Can you place the adverb in a different position in each sentence?

17. calmly

a. ____

____

b. ____

____

18. firmly

a. ____

____

b. ____

____

Adjectives

Remember those words that give you more information about a noun? Can you spot the five adjectives in this group? Write them underneath.

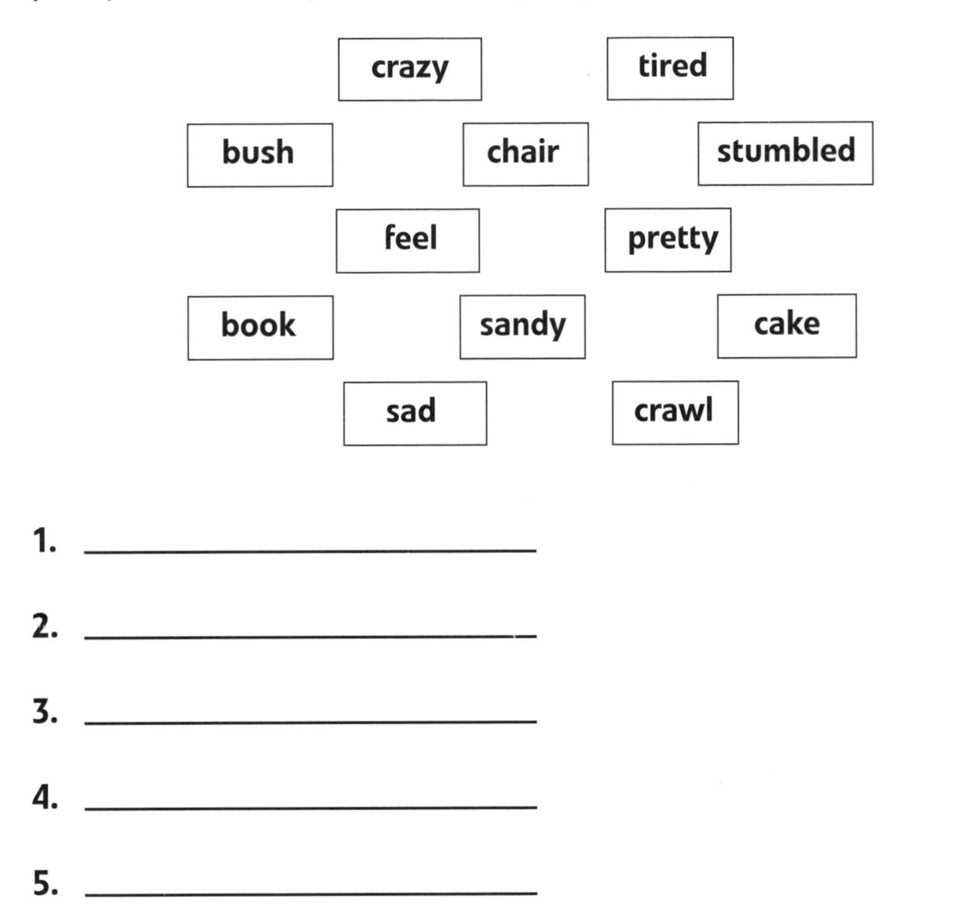

1. ______________________

2. ______________________

3. ______________________

4. ______________________

5. ______________________

Imagine a cat. Can you choose adjectives to describe it? Write one word next to each question.

6. What colour is it? ______________________

7. What does its fur feel like? ______________________

8. How could you describe its eyes? ______________________

9. How could you describe its claws? ______________________

10. What kind of mood is the cat in? ______________________

Grammar Revision

Alter these sentences so that the adjective is in a different position. Write the new sentence underneath. Remember: you might need to add some words to make a new sentence.

11. The clever child learnt his spellings.

____

____

12. The cat mewing loudly was black and white.

____

____

13. The angry child stamped his feet.

____

____

14. Charlie was the youngest member of the class.

____

____

15. Match the adjectives that have similar meanings.

generous	grumpy
noisy	kind
moody	ebony
tired	loud
black	fatigued
royal	fair
just	princely

Determiners

Read these sentences about hamsters. Circle the determiner in each sentence that tells the reader which hamster is being referred to.

1. Penny put her hamster down.

2. Penny and Jeffrey took their hamster to the vet.

3. Every hamster likes to chomp food.

4. I would like that hamster please, Mummy!

5. My hamster is sick.

6. Your hamster is a bit podgy.

7. I don't like any of these hamsters.

8. Our hamster slept for days and days.

9. The hamster washed his fur.

10. Each hamster costs £5.

Grammar Revision

Grammar summary

This section tests your knowledge of different word classes, e.g. nouns, adverbs, adjectives etc.

Read each sentence carefully and identify what type of word has been underlined. Group them in the boxes opposite.

1. That was a <u>good</u> effort.

2. That <u>was</u> a good effort.

3. The batsman <u>scored</u> one hundred runs.

4. The <u>batsman</u> scored one hundred runs.

5. <u>We</u> played happily all day.

6. We <u>played</u> happily all day.

7. We played <u>happily</u> all day.

8. Orange is a colour as well as a <u>fruit</u>.

9. Orange <u>is</u> a colour as well as a fruit.

10. <u>Hesitantly</u>, the man rose to his feet.

11. Hesitantly, the man <u>rose</u> to his feet.

12. Hesitantly, the man rose to <u>his</u> feet.

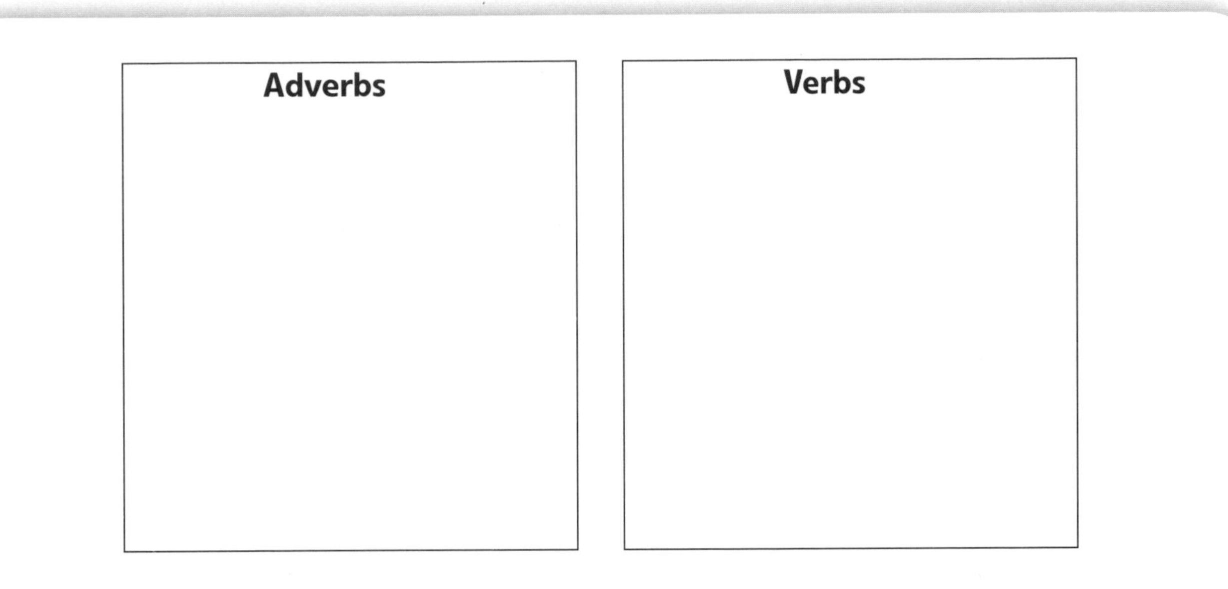

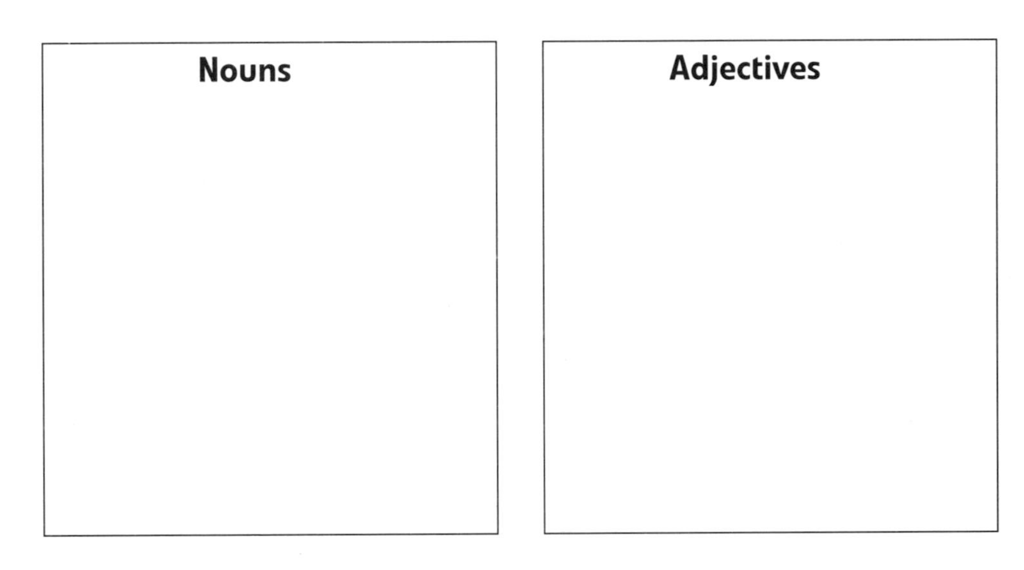

Determiners

Pronouns

Punctuation and Capital Letters

Punctuation is the term used for the marks we put down on paper to make sense of the words on a page.

Without punctuation there would be a continuous stream of words and it would be difficult to tell where one sentence or idea finished and another began. The text would be confusing and might not make sense.

There are several different punctuation marks, some of which are shown here:

FULL STOP	.
QUESTION MARK	?
EXCLAMATION MARK	!
COMMA	,
APOSTROPHE	'
SPEECH MARKS	" "

Capital letters

A sentence always begins with a capital letter.

★ **T**he food was very tasty.
★ **W**hat is the time?
★ **L**et's play a game.

Proper nouns (nouns that are the names of particular people, places, titles, or things) begin with a capital letter.

★ **S**am, **A**listair and **G**regory have visited many countries during their holidays: **E**ngland, **G**ermany, **F**rance, **G**reece and **I**taly. They have even seen **B**uckingham **P**alace and the **Q**ueen.

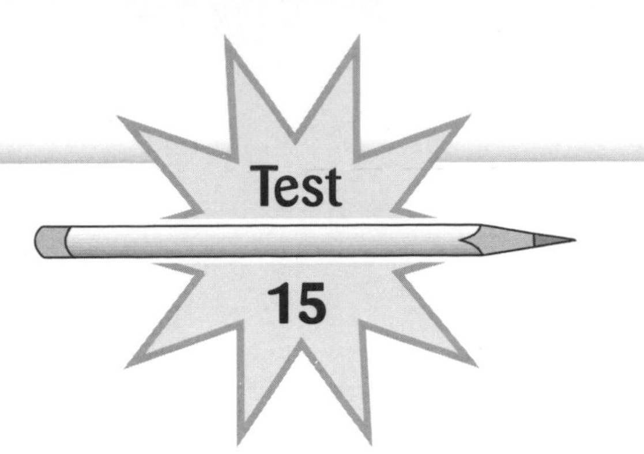

Cover up the opposite page and see if you can identify these punctuation marks.

1. . ____________

2. ’ ____________

3. ? ____________

4. “ ” ____________

5. , ____________

6. ! ____________

Something is wrong with these sentences. Copy the sentences, and make them correct.

7. the sun is shining. ____________

8. oranges are juicy. ____________

9. shall we go to the cinema? ____________

10. this is ridiculous! ____________

11. how are you? ____________

Now correct these sentences. The proper nouns need to start with a capital letter.

12. I will go shopping with amy and ian. ____________

13. We will take our holiday in june. ____________

14. sarah will be arriving on monday. ____________

15. Do you live in london? ____________

16. adam wants to meet the queen. ____________

Full Stops

A full stop looks like this: .

It is a round dot written at the end of a sentence.

★ She shouted loudly.

This is a complete sentence and it ends with a full stop.

When we read, a full stop tells us when to pause briefly. Without the full stops, we would get terribly out of breath when reading aloud! For example, try reading the following passage in which the full stops (and some capital letters) have been left out:

Red Riding Hood wants to take some flowers and cakes to her grandmother she bakes the cakes and picks the flowers on the way Red Riding Hood is spotted by the big bad wolf he decides to run to Grandma's home ahead of Red Riding Hood when Red Riding Hood arrives the big bad wolf is tucked up in Grandma's bed

Hard work, isn't it? Not only is it hard to read so many words without stopping for breath, but it is also difficult to make sense of what is happening. Now try again, taking a short pause when you see a full stop.

Red Riding Hood wants to take some flowers and cakes to her grandmother. She bakes the cakes and picks the flowers. On the way, Red Riding Hood is spotted by the big bad wolf. He decides to run to Grandma's home ahead of Red Riding Hood. When Red Riding Hood arrives, the big bad wolf is tucked up in Grandma's bed.

Much easier! This is why we use full stops.

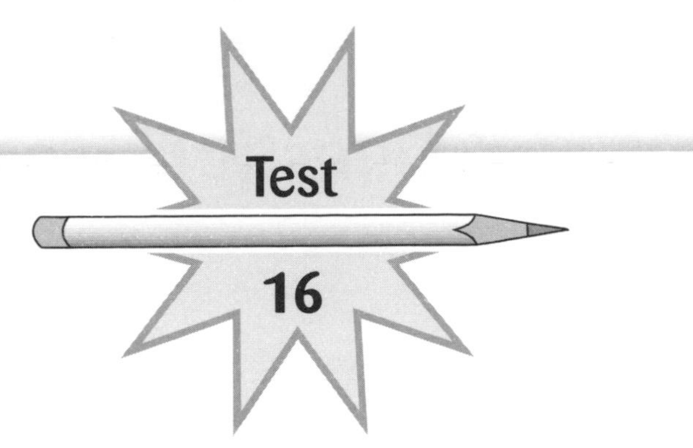

1. The computer has made an error and this piece of text has not been punctuated. The vertical lines separate the sentences. Can you rewrite the passage, beginning each sentence with a capital letter and ending with a full stop?

peter wanted a bike | he wanted to buy the one in the shop | he didn't have enough money | he decided to ask his dad | his dad told him he could buy it on his birthday |

____

____

____

____

____

____

2. Now try this one. Separate the sentences with a vertical line. Then write the new passage underneath.

sally looked for her cat she couldn't find it anywhere suddenly she saw the tip of a ginger tail behind a plant pot she crept up to the pot it wasn't her cat it was a kitten then she saw a pair of ears sticking out from under the table it was her cat Ginger

____

____

____

____

____

____

Exclamation and Question Marks

Exclamation mark

An exclamation mark – **!** – is a full stop with a vertical line above it. There is a small space between the line and the circle.

When you want to show that someone is speaking with strong feeling, you end the sentence with an exclamation mark.

- ★ Watch out, the tree is falling down**!**
- ★ What an amazing place this is**!**
- ★ Help me**!**
- ★ Stop**!**

Question mark

A question mark looks like this: **?**

Questions are sentences that need answers. They begin with a capital letter and end with a question mark.

Often, questions begin with question words such as these:

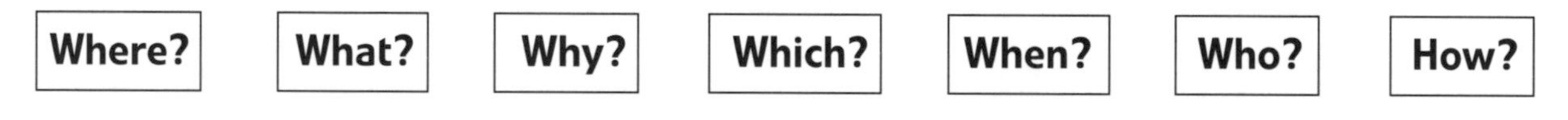

But sometimes questions do not begin with a question word. Here are some examples of questions. Can you spot the ones that don't begin with question words?

- ★ Have you eaten my toffee**?**
- ★ Where is my coat**?**
- ★ Can I borrow a book**?**
- ★ Do I look nice in this jumper**?**
- ★ What is the time**?**
- ★ Which film did you see**?**
- ★ When will you be home**?**
- ★ Can you hear music**?**
- ★ Is this a good film**?**
- ★ Will Arsenal win on Saturday**?**

However, regardless of whether a question begins with a question word or not, it must ***always*** end with a question mark.

1. Match these question words to the rest of their question.

What	is coming to dinner tonight?
Where	biscuit would you prefer?
When	will dad be home?
How	time is Blue Peter on TV?
Who	did they put the salt?
Which	many toys do you have?

Write either a question mark or an exclamation mark after each sentence.

2. Are you hungry _

3. Will they be pleased _

4. Help – the house is on fire _

5. Are you running in the marathon _

6. Is Robyn the tallest in the class _

7. Where is the post office _

8. I love you more than ever _

9. What do you mean _

10. That is absolutely amazing _

11. Who was that girl _

12. I've won first prize _

13. How long will it take _

14. Stop that thief _

15. What is your favourite film _

16. I can't believe my luck _

17. Where is my sister _

Commas

A comma is a punctuation mark which looks like this: ,

When writing a comma, it should be positioned on the line and is like a full stop with a small flick down and to the left.

Commas have lots of uses:

Commas are used to separate items in a list, for example, when listing names or objects.

★ I need apples, bananas, carrots, cabbages, damsons and plums.
★ My friends are Sarah, Jo, Toby, Helen and Sue.

(Note: Usually commas are not used before *and* in a list.)

Commas are used to show the reader where to pause in a sentence. Often the comma separates a phrase that gives more information from the main clause.

★ Although it's late, I'll help you.
★ Laughing loudly, Mary jumped on the trampoline.
★ Jane, my teacher, is nice.
★ Richard, the engineer, will be arriving soon.

Commas are used to mark off the person being addressed.

★ Sarah, wait for me.
★ Peter, I love you.
★ Stop, you fool, or you'll break it!

When deciding where to place a comma in your writing, it is very helpful to read your sentences aloud. Listen out for when you would naturally take a short break. That is probably where you need to put your comma.

Separate the items in these lists using commas. Think carefully about how to punctuate if there is an "and" before the last item.

1. I need to buy bananas crisps apples milk butter eggs and ham.
2. Beckham Giggs Scholes Butt and Neville are my favourite players.
3. For the school play we would like white shirts black plimsolls blue trousers and a red scarf.
4. Pupils should bring pencils pens a ruler a rubber a pencil sharpener and a pair of compasses.
5. In my suitcase I must put sunglasses underwear a towel toothpaste and a toothbrush.
6. I went home ate my tea had a bath and watched television.

Decide which information could be separated out using a comma and write the new sentence on the line. The first one has been done for you.

7. Sally our mum is a teacher. Sally, our mum, is a teacher.
8. I met Billy your brother at the pool. ________________
9. Although I was tired I stayed up late. ________________
10. Blake the head boy spoke at assembly. ________________
11. Putting on her socks Sarah sang a tune. ________________
12. Alex a toddler cheered the clown. ________________
13. If you don't hurry we'll be late. ________________

Possessive Apostrophes

The apostrophe looks just like a comma but, rather than sitting on the line, it's always in line with the top of the letters – **'**

The apostrophe has two uses:

1) **It is used to show possession.**
2) **It is used to show that letters have been missed out of a word.**

How an apostrophe shows possession

The apostrophe can be used to show ownership, i.e. who an item belongs to or is part of. We use it at the end of a word with an **s**, like this, **'s** .

It means **of** or **belonging to**.

For example:

★ the dog**'s** tail	(this has the same meaning as: the tail of the dog)
★ the boy**'s** book	(the book of the boy)
★ the cat**'s** tooth	(the tooth of the cat)
★ Tom**'s** video game	(the video game of Tom)

IMPORTANT NOTE!

Care must be taken not to misuse the apostrophe. It should **not** be used for plurals.

For example:

★ The lady bought two pear's.	**WRONG!**
★ The lady bought two pears.	**RIGHT!**

Test 19

Change these possessive words into their longer form:

1. the rabbit's skin ___the skin of the rabbit___
2. Mary's book ______________________
3. the dog's bark ______________________
4. John's voice ______________________
5. the footballer's success ______________________

Use the possessive apostrophe to correct the underlined word and write it in the box.

6. This boys hands are filthy. [boy's]
7. Saturdays match was a disaster. [ ]
8. The brides mother cried. [ ]
9. Your sisters friend is kind. [ ]
10. My Dads snooker cue snapped. [ ]

Read these sentences. Write "possessive" if the underlined word is possessive and "plural" if it is a plural of a noun.

11. The apples were ripe. [plural]
12. The boy's sweets had gone. [ ]
13. The girl's skirt is too short. [ ]
14. That is my friend's dog. [ ]
15. You can buy oranges at the corner shop. [ ]

Possessive Apostrophes 2

Singular and plural forms

If the noun is **singular**, you add an apostrophe and an **s** to show possession.

★ The girl**'s** coat.
(The apostrophe ***before*** the ***s*** shows the coat belongs to just ***one*** girl.)

If the noun is **plural** and ***already ends*** in **s**, you just add the apostrophe after the **s**.

★ The boys**'** trophy.
(The apostrophe ***after*** the ***s*** shows that the trophy belongs to ***more than one*** boy.)

If the noun is **plural** but does ***not*** end in **s**, you add an apostrophe and an **s**.

★ The women**'s** hats. (the hats of the women)
★ The mice**'s** tails. (the tails of the mice)
★ The men**'s** tools. (the tools of the men)

Names that end in s

As you know, some names end in **s**. For example: James, Charles, Francis. In such a case we can either add an apostrophe or we can add an apostrophe plus an extra **s**.

★ James**'** or James**'s** head. (the head of James)
★ Charles**'** or Charles**'s** voice. (the voice of Charles)
★ Francis**'** or Francis**'s** coat. (the coat of Francis)

Test 20

State whether these possessive nouns are singular or plural:

1a. the girl's jewellery ______singular______
b. the girls' jewellery ______plural______

2a. the cats' food ____________
b. the cat's food ____________

3a. the boy's jeans ____________
b. the boys' jeans ____________

4a. the elephant's ears ____________
b. the elephants' ears ____________

Change the following into the possessive form:

5. the hat of James ____________

6. the hair of Francis ____________

7. the car of Charles ____________

8. the skirts of the women ____________

9. the tails of the dogs ____________

Not all of these sentences are correct. Tick the sentences in which the apostrophe has been used correctly.

10. The mans' car had broken down. ☐

11. The cat's dish had been lost. ☐

12. Lewis' coat hung on the peg. ☐

13. What happened to Marys' mother? ☐

Apostrophes of Contractions

How apostrophes show missing letters

The other way in which we use apostrophes is to show that some letters have been missed out of a word or words.

When metal contracts, it gets shorter. Similarly, when words contract (i.e. when they get pushed together to sound like one word) they become shorter, that is, some of the letters get missed out.

For example, when we are talking, only a very precise and well-spoken person would say:

"I am not in a good mood today. I do not feel like going to school. It is not fair."

Most of us would say:

"**I'm** not in a good mood today. I **don't** feel like going to school. **It's** not fair."

I am	has become	**I'm**	An **a** has been left out
do not	has become	**don't**	An **o** has been left out
it is	has become	**it's**	An **i** has been left out

We can see then that the apostrophe shows us where we have missed out some letters.

Here are more examples of some common contractions:

I will – I'll
will not – won't
is not – isn't
I would – I'd
she would or had – she'd

I have – I've
you will – you'll
he is or has – he's
they are – they're
you have – you've

Can you see which letters have been missed out?

REMEMBER!

Remember not to mix up **it's** and **its**!

- **its** means something **belonging to it** and there's ***no*** apostrophe.
- **it's** is short for **it is** and there ***is*** an apostrophe.

★ **It's** time for the cat to have **its** dinner.

Test 21

Write the expanded form of these contractions:

1.	I'll	I will	**4.**	you'll	________
2.	she'd	________	**5.**	he's	________
3.	won't	________	**6.**	I'm	________

Write the contracted forms of these words:

7.	I would	I'd	**11.**	do not	________
8.	I am	________	**12.**	is not	________
9.	it is	________	**13.**	they are	________
10.	you have	________	**14.**	I have	________

Choose the contraction that makes sense and write it in the space.

don't	I've	they're	it's	won't

15. ________ always been good at sports.

16. The sign says," ________ smoke."

17. "I ________ go to bed!" shouted the boy.

18. ________ time to go home.

19. ________ going for their walk.

20. "________ forget to post my letter," said Sue.

Speech Marks

Speech marks are used to punctuate **direct speech**. In direct speech, the words are written **as a person said or says them**. The speech marks show when the person begins speaking and when they stop speaking. For example, look at Robyn:

In text this would be written as:

★ Robyn said, **"I won first prize."**

The **bold type** shows what Robyn actually said, wrapped around by speech marks, which look like this: **" "**

What Robyn said is a complete sentence, and is punctuated as a sentence, within the speech marks.

To use speech marks, follow these four easy steps:

1) Open the speech marks: "
2) Write the words that were spoken: "I won first prize
3) Add **! ? ,** or **.** : "I won first prize.
4) Close the speech marks: "I won first prize."

Notice how when the speaker appears **before** the speech, a comma must be placed before the speech marks.

★ Robyn said, "I won first prize."

When the speaker appears **after** the speech, the spoken words are followed by a **comma**, *not a full stop.*

★ "I won first prize," said Robyn.

If the spoken words are a question or an exclamation, we use a **question mark or an exclamation mark**, whether the speaker comes before or after the speech.

★ "Did I win?" asked Robyn.
★ "I came first!" shouted Robyn.
★ Robyn asked, "Did I win?"
★ Robyn shouted, "I came first!"

Punctuate these examples of direct speech by putting speech marks in the correct places. Copy the new sentence on to the line below. The first one has been done for you.

1. Robert asked, Is it time for tea?

   Robert asked, "Is it time for tea?"

2. Ben muttered, It's not fair.

   ____

3. I need some new shoes, said the old lady.

   ____

4. Can you direct me to the hospital? asked the driver.

   ____

5. I wish I hadn't come, moaned Fiona. I should have stayed in bed.

   ____

6. Who would like a balloon? asked the clown.

   ____

7. He made a rabbit disappear! gasped Annie.

   ____

Punctuation Revision

In this section your knowledge of punctuation will be put to the test.

Punctuating a sentence

This section revises your knowledge of how to punctuate sentences using different punctuation marks.

In each of these sentences you will need to check that the capital letter is in the correct place. Write the corrected sentence alongside.

1. cats can Be fluffy and soft. ______________________________

2. sometimes we enjoy doing Our homework. ______________________________

3. school Ends at three o'clock. ______________________________

4. stop Doing that! ______________________________

Look at these sentences carefully and add capital letters where they're needed. You may have to add more than one capital letter, so concentrate!

5. my favourite lesson is english. ______________________________

6. my sister's name is cathy. ______________________________

7. why is john crying? ______________________________

8. her birthday is in december. ______________________________

9. i like cake and i like biscuits. ______________________________

10. There are two different purposes for which capital letters are used. Look at the examples above to help you identify them. Complete the table below to show when you use capital letters and write an example for each.

You use capital letters for…	**An example is…**

11. The author who wrote this passage is confused about where to put full stops and capital letters in her sentences. Check her work and write the corrected passage underneath.

goldilocks lowered herself onto the chair and boy did she get a shock the chair collapsed underneath her leaving her sprawling on the floor however she was not to be beaten and so she climbed the creaky stairs to the top of the house what she found were three different sized rooms, each with their own bed "excellent," she thought to herself "now i can get a proper rest"

____

____

____

____

____

____

____

____

____

____

Add the correct punctuation mark to the end of each sentence. Choose from: a full stop, a question mark and an exclamation mark.

12. What time is it ___

13. I went to the fair yesterday ___

14. I won't do it ___

15. My favourite sport is swimming ___

16. Did you have a good weekend ___

17. Why did you do that ___

Punctuation Revision

18. Generally, I don't watch sport ___

19. Come here now ___

20. Ouch ___

21. Who are you ___

22. When do we use a question mark?

____

____

23. When do we use an exclamation mark?

____

____

Write the questions for these answers:

24. Q. ____

A. We have assembly after lunch.

25. Q. ____

A. We play football on Wednesdays.

26. Q. ____

A. I made my musical instrument with Jane.

27. Q. ____

A. Yes, I enjoy coming to school.

28. Q. ____

A. There are one hundred centimetres in a metre.

Write the appropriate question word in the space provided.

who	where	when	what	which

29. ____________________ is the sum of ten and two?

30. ____________________ wrote that book?

31. ____________________ is my pencil?

32. ____________________ do you prefer – chocolate or cake?

33. ____________________ are we going home?

Read each sentence, paying attention to the commas. Tick each sentence in which commas have been used correctly. Add any commas that are missing.

34. I packed my sleeping bag, toothbrush, alarm clock and book. ☐

35. My sister is ugly annoying and rude. ☐

36. We plan to travel to Africa, America New Zealand and Australia. ☐

37. The shopping list included milk, bread and, cheese. ☐

Each of these sentences needs at least one comma. Write the new sentence on the next line.

38. The naughty girl Goldilocks knocked on the door.

____

39. Greedily she ate the porridge.

____

40. Climbing up the stairs Goldilocks sighed to herself.

____

Punctuation Revision

Apostrophes

We use apostrophes to show that some letters have been missed out of a word or words.

Write a sentence for each contracted word.

1. can't ______

2. won't ______

3. don't ______

4. isn't ______

5. he's ______

6. Complete this table. The first line has been done for you.

Word	Contracted version
do not	don't
let us	
did not	
I am	
can not	

Write these sentences, placing the apostrophe in the correct place:

7. It is not raining now. ______

8. We will be late if we do not hurry. ______

9. Linda will not tell us what she is making. ______

10. We are sure she saw us. ______

11. I am feeling tired today. ______

Read each sentence carefully and decide whether **its** or **it's** is needed.

12. The cat did not eat _______ dinner.

13. _______ horrible when you have no friends.

14. _______ important to brush your teeth at least twice a day.

15. _______ not fair!

16. The book stood on _______ stand.

17. Complete this table. The first line has been done for you.

Possessive words	**Words in their longer form**
Jenny's pencil	the pencil of Jenny
the cat's whiskers	
	the bag of Susan
	the beard of the man
Paul's umbrella	
the teacher's glasses	
	the brush of the woman
the frog's legs	
	the cake of Mary
the boy's sweets	

State whether these possessive nouns are singular or plural:

18. the boy's name _______________

19. the man's car _______________

20. the boys' coats _______________

21. the child's book _______________

22. the teachers' registers _______________

Punctuation Revision

Speech marks

Punctuate these examples of direct speech by putting speech marks in the correct place.

1. Give that to me, said John.
2. I don't know, replied the boy.
3. Who would like a cup of tea? the secretary asked.
4. Steven whispered, What did you say?
5. Jamie gasped, Oh no, not again!

For these sentences you will need to think carefully about where to place the speech marks. Write the new sentences below.

6. Oh no, moaned Peter, you'll never guess what I've done.

____

7. Come inside at once, said Dad. You're late as it is.

____

8. Please mum, said Mark, can I go to Stephen's house?

____

9. Yes, I did eat all the cake, admitted Andrew, but I was very hungry.

____

10. Have you seen my dog? the old man inquired. It ran off early this morning.

____

Punctuation summary

1. Now, using everything you have learnt, punctuate this text. Write the corrected version in the space provided.

listen to me class i have something interesting to tell you began miss black we are going on a trip next tuesday to the roman villa excellent chorused the class they listened carefully as miss black explained the kinds of activities they would be doing she told them about the roman artefacts they would see the tour of the villa and the treasure hunt they would enjoy after lunch can we bring our own packed lunch asked paul im going to have a wagon wheel exclaimed one girl you can bring whatever you like – its totally up to you concluded miss black

Alphabetical Order

Putting words in alphabetical order helps us to find information easily from books, indexes and dictionaries.

The 26 letters of the alphabet are always in the same order, and every word in the English language uses them.

Here they are:

a b c d e f g h i j k l
m n o p q r s t u v w x
y z

Putting words in order

If you are asked to put a group of words into alphabetical order, the **first letter** of each word will usually tell you its position. So:

Barry, David and Adam will appear in alphabetical order as:
★ **A**dam, **B**arry and **D**avid.

If several words begin with the same letter you have to take the **second letter** into account. So:

axe, animal and apple will appear in alphabetical order as:
★ a**n**imal, a**p**ple, a**x**e

Using a dictionary

When you are reading a book, a magazine or a paper, you may come across words you don't understand. When this happens you can look them up in a dictionary. **A dictionary is a book in which words are listed alphabetically and their meanings explained.**

Knowing the order of the alphabet means that you will be able to find the meaning of any word.

Test 23

Put each of these words into alphabetical order. Look at the first letter.

1. dog ant zebra lion elephant

____

2. girl boy man lady child

____

3. flower seed grow pond hat

____

Put each of these words into alphabetical order. Look at the second letter.

4. crisps corn cider cheese cabbage

____

5. sea sun sand starfish spade

____

6. oven out on off olive

____

Use your dictionary to find out what these words mean. Write the explanation in the space provided.

7. ordinary ______________________________

8. bungalow ______________________________

9. pride ______________________________

10. dictionary ______________________________

11. container ______________________________

Homophones and Homonyms

Homophones

Homophones are words that **sound the same**. They have **different spellings** and **different meanings**.

For example:

★ The **sun** set over the ocean.
★ The **son** gave his father a card.

Other examples of homophones are:

witch	**which**
stare	**stair**
hair	**hare**
hour	**our**
meddle	**medal**
deer	**dear**

You can use a dictionary to find out the correct spellings and the meanings.

Homonyms

Homonyms are words that **sound the same** and are **spelt the same**, but have **different meanings**.

For example:

★ The conductor will **bow** to the audience.
★ The captain stood on the **bow** of the ship.

Other examples of homonyms are:

iron	(ironing)	**iron**	(metal)
jumper	(clothes)	**jumper**	(person who jumps)
present	(gift)	**present**	(here, now)
will	(resolve)	**will**	(legacy)

Again, your dictionary will tell you if a word has more than one meaning.

Complete the sentences using the correct word from the brackets. Use a dictionary if you need to.

1. There were ______________ children in the shop. (to, two, too)
2. The boys wanted to ______________ the boat across the pond. (sale, sail)
3. We waited an ______________ for the train. (hour, our)
4. The child paddled with ______________ feet. (bare, bear)
5. The ______________ of the shoe needed mending. (heal, heel)
6. The ______________ took off from the airport. (plain, plane)
7. The man could not ______________ the doorbell. (here, hear)
8. The lady had her ______________ cut. (hair, hare)

Use a dictionary to look up these homonyms. Write two sentences for each word explaining its different meanings. The first one has been done for you.

9. bank A business that looks after people's money.
   The raised ground along the edge of a river or lake.
10. letter ______________________________
    ____
11. ring ______________________________
    ____
12. race ______________________________
    ____
13. watch ______________________________
    ____

Spelling Singular and Plural Nouns

Singular and plural nouns

A singular noun refers to a single thing or person and a plural noun refers to more than one thing or person.

★ one dog
★ one book

★ two dogs
★ a few books

Making plural nouns

In most cases, you can make a plural noun by adding 's' on to the end of a singular noun. So:

★ dog becomes dogs
★ book becomes books

However, there are some exceptions to this rule. Here are a few patterns:

IF THE WORD ENDS IN:	DO THIS:	AND ADD:	FOR EXAMPLE:
ch **s** **sh** **x** **z**	nothing	**es**	church ... churches dish ... dishes box ... boxes
f **fe**	change the **f** or **fe** for **v**	**es**	calf ... calves wolf ... wolves wife ... wives knife ... knives **Note: there are exceptions:** belief ... beliefs roof ... roofs proof ... proofs
consonant + y	change the **y** to **i**	**es**	baby ... babies country ... countries lady ... ladies

NOTE: There are exceptions to these patterns so it is always wise to check in the dictionary if you are at all unsure.

Nouns that take a new form in the plural

Some nouns have a completely different plural form.

★ One child ... many children
★ One person ... many people
★ One mouse ... many mice

1. Can you make these words into their plural, so that there is a sack of goodies for all to share? The first one has been done for you.

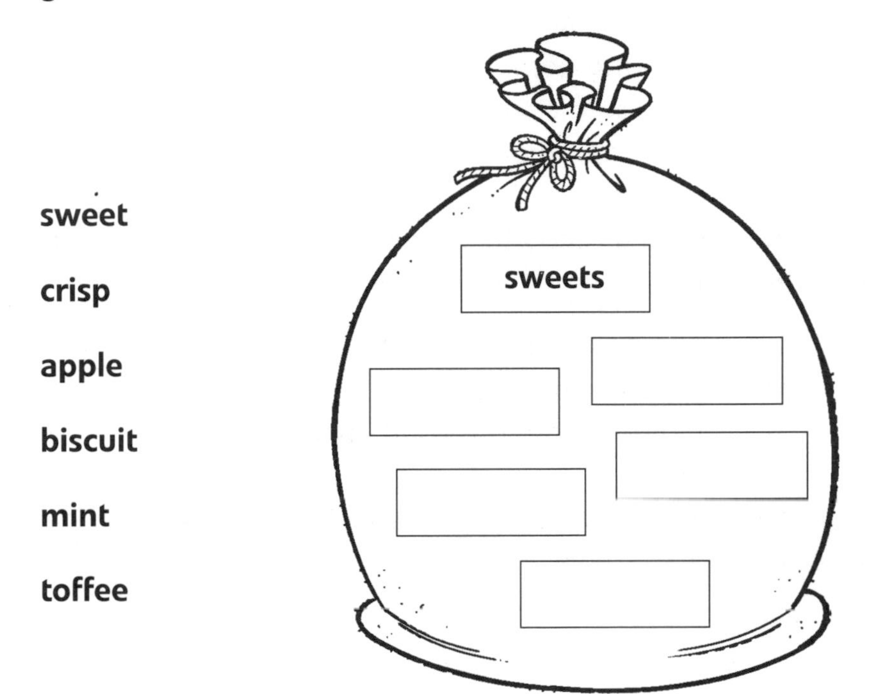

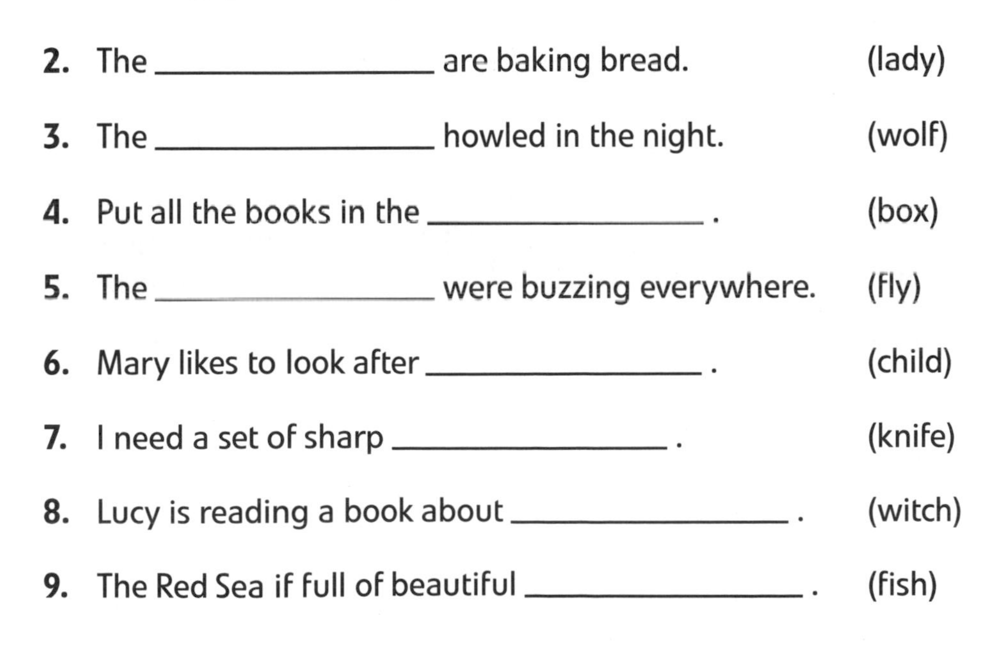

Fill in the gap with the plural form of the noun in brackets.

2. The ________________ are baking bread. (lady)
3. The ________________ howled in the night. (wolf)
4. Put all the books in the ________________ . (box)
5. The ________________ were buzzing everywhere. (fly)
6. Mary likes to look after ________________ . (child)
7. I need a set of sharp ________________ . (knife)
8. Lucy is reading a book about ________________ . (witch)
9. The Red Sea if full of beautiful ________________ . (fish)

Suffixes: -ing, -ed

A verb is a part of speech that tells you what a person or thing does or how they are. The **endings** or **suffixes** which are added to verbs change depending upon when the action is taking place.

We use **ing** at the end of a verb to describe what someone is doing **right now**.

For example:

★ walk Mary is walk**ing** home.
★ cook Tom is cook**ing** the supper.
★ jump The dog is jump**ing** on the sofa.

If we talk about an action that has **already happened**, we put it in the past tense. To do this we write **ed** at the end of the verb.

★ walk Mary walk**ed** to school yesterday.
★ cook Tom cook**ed** lunch last week.
★ jump The dog jump**ed** into the pond on Saturday.

Usually, if the verb has a long vowel sound, you may just add **ing/ed** to the end of the base verb. Here are some more examples:

★ play playing played
★ talk talking talked
★ bark barking barked
★ look looking looked

There are, however, exceptions to this rule. Here are some other patterns:

IF THE BASE VERB ENDS IN:	DO THIS:	AND ADD:	FOR EXAMPLE:
A short vowel sound	double the last letter	**ing** or **ed**	stop stopping stopped hop hopping hopped drop dropping dropped
y (when adding **ing**) **y** (when adding **ed**)	nothing change the **y** to an **i**	**ing** **ed**	try trying tried cry crying cried fry frying fried
e	remove the **e**	**ing** or **ed**	stare staring stared live living lived hope hoping hoped close closing closed

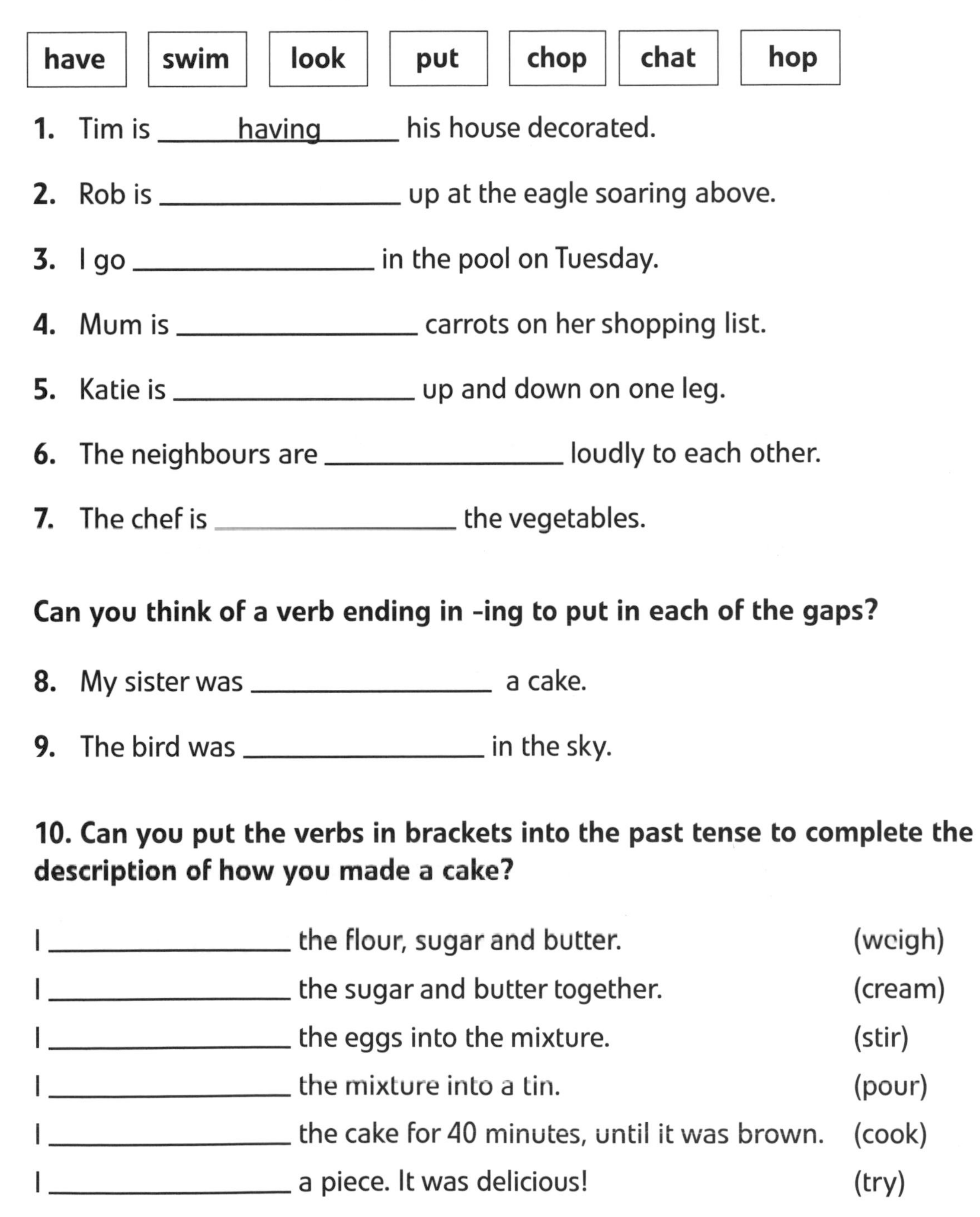

Choose the correct word to put into the sentences. Add -ing to show that the actions are happening now. The first one has been done for you.

have	swim	look	put	chop	chat	hop

1. Tim is ___having___ his house decorated.
2. Rob is ________________ up at the eagle soaring above.
3. I go ________________ in the pool on Tuesday.
4. Mum is ________________ carrots on her shopping list.
5. Katie is ________________ up and down on one leg.
6. The neighbours are ________________ loudly to each other.
7. The chef is ________________ the vegetables.

Can you think of a verb ending in -ing to put in each of the gaps?

8. My sister was ________________ a cake.
9. The bird was ________________ in the sky.

10. Can you put the verbs in brackets into the past tense to complete the description of how you made a cake?

I ________________ the flour, sugar and butter.	(weigh)
I ________________ the sugar and butter together.	(cream)
I ________________ the eggs into the mixture.	(stir)
I ________________ the mixture into a tin.	(pour)
I ________________ the cake for 40 minutes, until it was brown.	(cook)
I ________________ a piece. It was delicious!	(try)

Suffixes: -able, -ible

Many words end in -able and -ible. Sometimes it is hard to remember which one to use. The **-ible** ending is for words that have a Latin origin. Latin is an old language that is no longer used. However, it used to be the language spoken by the Romans a long time ago and has formed the basis of many current languages. The **-able** ending is used for non-Latin words. Over the years, there have been new words added such as: networkable.

Here is a little rule to help you decide the correct spelling. It works in most cases:

★ **If you remove -ible from a word, you are not left with a complete word.**

For example:

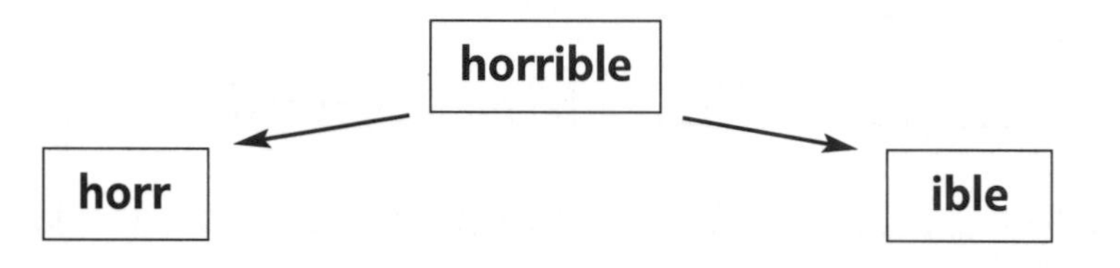

If we remove the suffix **-ible**, we are left with **horr**, which is not a recognisable word.

★ **If you remove -able from a word, you are left with a complete word.**

For example:

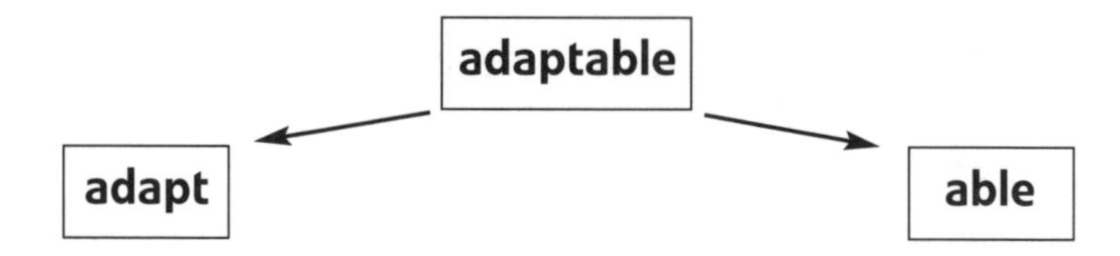

If we remove the suffix **-able**, we are left with the word **adapt**.

You can use this rule most of the time, but remember – if you are not sure about a word, it is always best to use a dictionary.

Test 27

Add -able or -ible to complete these words:

1. poss _ _ _ _
2. suit _ _ _ _
3. sens _ _ _ _
4. invis _ _ _ _
5. fashion _ _ _ _
6. comfort _ _ _ _
7. terr _ _ _ _
8. enjoy _ _ _ _

Complete these sentences, choosing from the words above. N.B. You may be able to use more than one word to complete a sentence.

9. Is it ____________________ to run that fast?
10. The dress was very ____________________ .
11. The teacher said that the children were very ____________________ on their school trip.
12. The weather that weekend was ____________________ . It didn't stop raining!
13. These clothes are not ____________________ for a wedding. They are too scruffy.
14. The wizard made himself ____________________ when he didn't want to be seen.
15. The chair was not ____________________ .
16. The children found the trip to the cinema very ____________________ .
17. Is it ____________________ to see the sun at night?

Suffixes: -er and -est

Sometimes we use adjectives to compare people or things. We call such adjectives comparatives or superlatives.

Comparative adjectives

We use a comparative adjective to say that a person or thing has **more of a certain quality than another person or thing**.

For example:

★ Paul is **taller** than Christopher.
★ This biscuit is **smaller** than that one.

It is usually formed by adding **er** to a word:

★ short shorter
★ long longer

Or by putting **more** before the word:

★ beautiful more beautiful
★ exciting more exciting

Superlative adjectives

We use a superlative adjective to say that a person or thing has **more of a certain quality than all the other people or things in a group or a category**.

For example:

★ Paul is the **tallest** boy in the class.
★ This is the **smallest** biscuit in the packet.

It is usually formed by adding **est** to a word:

★ short shortest
★ long longest

Or by putting **most** before the word:

★ beautiful most beautiful
★ exciting most exciting

There are a few patterns that may help when spelling comparatives and superlatives:

IF THE ADJECTIVE ENDS IN:	DO THIS:	ADD:	FOR EXAMPLE:
consonant-vowel-consonant	double the last letter	**er** **est**	sad sadder saddest
consonant + e	remove the **e**		wide wider widest
consonant + y	change the **y** to an **i**		happy happier happiest

1. Can you change the following words into comparatives and superlatives? The first one has been done for you.

	COMPARATIVES	SUPERLATIVES
light	lighter	lightest
tall		
full		
dark		
soft		
old		
slow		
fast		
high		
low		
fat		
thin		
cold		
hot		
sad		
wide		
happy		
dry		

Complete the sentences so that they make sense.

2. It has been the ______________ day of the year. (hotter/hottest)

3. That is the ______________ medal I have ever seen. (shinier/shiniest)

4. This apple is ______________ than yours. (bigger/biggest)

5. This is the ______________ pie I have ever eaten. (tastier/tastiest)

Suffixes: -tion, -sion, -cian

Many English nouns end with the sound "**-shun**", which can be spelt in different ways.

-tion

By far the most common spelling for this ending is **-tion**.

Use -tion at the end of a word if the word ends in the sound t.

★ ac**t**	ac**tion**
★ rela**te**	rela**tion**
★ disse**ct**	dissec**tion**

Use -tion if the sound comes after a long vowel.

- ★ combina**tion**
- ★ vaca**tion**
- ★ comple**tion**
- ★ po**tion**

Use -tion immediately after a short i.

- ★ perdi**tion**
- ★ defini**tion**
- ★ condi**tion**

-sion

Nouns ending in -sion usually come from verbs with the endings nd, ge, and vert.

★ apprehe**nd**	apprehen**sion**
★ submer**ge**	submer**sion**
★ di**vert**	diver**sion**

-cian

Use -cian when referring to people.

★ magic	magi**cian**
★ music	musi**cian**
★ politics	politi**cian**

Can you complete the following words using the appropriate suffixes: -tion, -sion or -cian? Use a dictionary to check the spellings of the words you have formed.

1. libera _ _ _ _

2. posi _ _ _ _

3. musi _ _ _ _

4. informa _ _ _ _

5. na _ _ _ _

6. combina _ _ _ _

7. diver _ _ _ _

8. mathemati _ _ _ _

9. situa _ _ _ _

10. peti _ _ _ _

11. politi _ _ _ _

12. quota _ _ _ _

13. educa _ _ _ _

14. qualifica _ _ _ _

15. magi _ _ _ _

16. occupa _ _ _ _

17. punctua _ _ _ _

18. associa _ _ _ _

19. exclama _ _ _ _

20. depriva _ _ _ _

Add -tion or -cian to these and then complete the sentences that follow.

electri _ _ _ _ **popula _ _ _ _** **imagina _ _ _ _** **competi _ _ _ _**

21. It was a difficult ____________________ but I won.

22. The ____________________ of the world continues to grow.

23. The lights went out so we called an ____________________ .

24. The author had a good ____________________ . The plot was very exciting.

Suffixes: -ful, -less and -ly

You will remember that a suffix is a group of letters that we add to the end of a root word to make a new word.

-ly, **-ful** and **-less** are some of the most common suffixes. Look at the examples below.

-ful

root word		suffix		new word
hope	+	**ful**	=	**hopeful**

"Hopeful" means "full of hope". You will notice that the suffix **-ful** does not have a double l.

-less

root word		suffix		new word
hope	+	**less**	=	**hopeless**

"Hopeless" means "without hope".

-ly

The suffix **-ly** is added to an adjective or verb to create an adverb. Look at the example below.

root word		suffix		new word
proud	+	**ly**	=	**proudly**

★ The man walked **proudly** across the room.

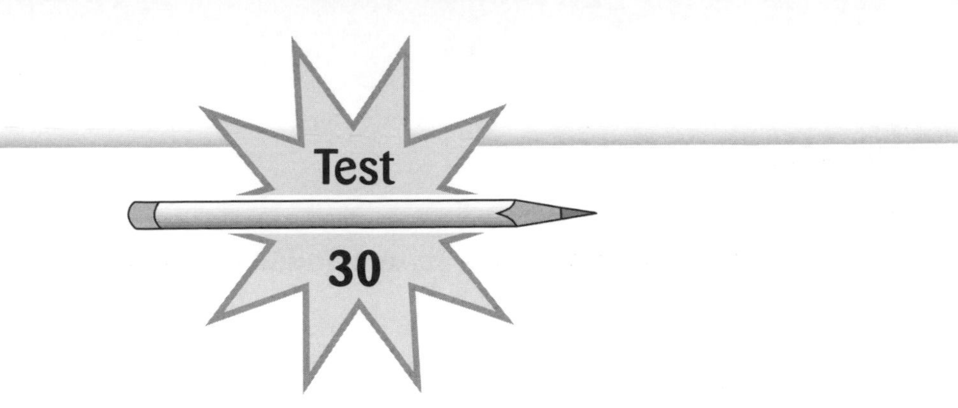

Look at each root word and see how many new words you can make using the suffixes **-ful**, **-less** and **-ly**. Check your words by looking in a dictionary and write them on the lines provided.

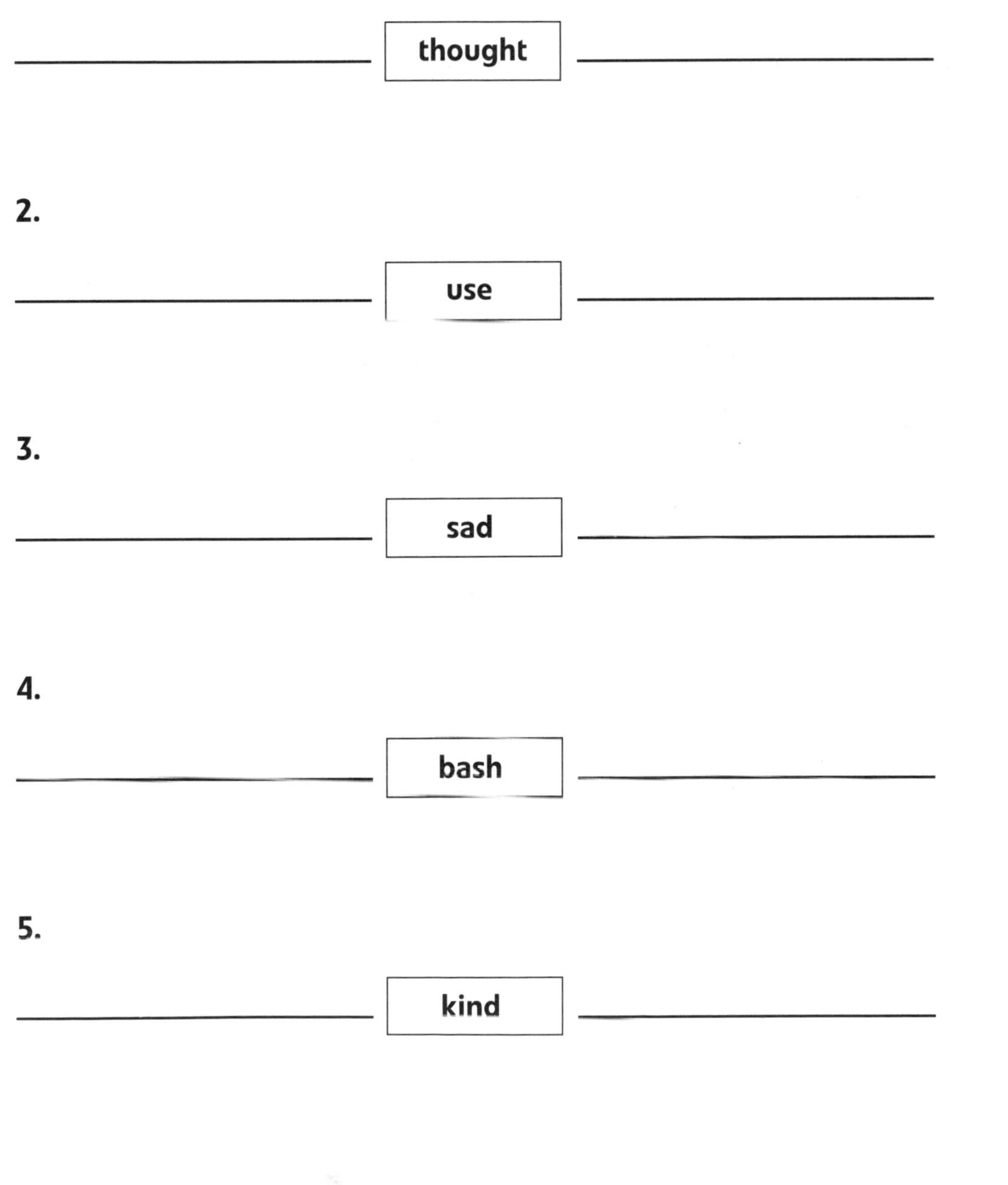

Prefixes

A prefix is a letter or a group of letters added to the beginning of a root word to make a new word.

Once you identify the prefix, it provides a clue about the meaning of the word. For example, the prefix "un" means "not", so "unhappy" means "not happy".

Some prefixes can be added to create an opposite to the original root word in this way.

Here are some more examples:

PREFIX	ROOT WORD	NEW WORD
un	kind	unkind
un	do	undo

Here are some of the most common prefixes and their meanings:

PREFIX	MEANING	EXAMPLES
de	make the opposite of	deform decode
dis	not/the opposite of	dislike disinfect
re	again	rebuild refill
mis	wrong/false	miscount misbehave
non	not/opposite of	non-stick nonsense
co	joint/together	co-star
anti	against	anti-clockwise
sub	under	submarine subway
mini	small	minibus
ex	out/outside of	export

Can you add the correct prefix – -dis or -un – to create opposites for these words? Write the new word on the line.

1. even ______________

2. honest ______________

3. healthy ______________

4. wrap ______________

5. obey ______________

6. fortunate ______________

7. known ______________

8. trust ______________

9. approve ______________

10. fair ______________

11. Can you match these words to the prefixes by sorting them into the correct boxes? Watch out for words that can be put into two boxes!

understood **skirt** **design**
certain **fiction** **read** **write**
stop **fuse** **usual**

mis	**re**

non	**un**

mini	**de**

Discriminating Syllables

Words are made up of sounds, or syllables. Every word will have one, two, three, or more syllables. Nearly every syllable will contain at least one vowel (a, e, i, o, u) or vowel sound.

For example:

★ **Cat** is a word with **one** syllable.

★ **Rabbit** is a word with **two** syllables.

We can separate the sounds in the word like this: **rabb** **it**

★ **Crocodile** is a word with **three** syllables:

We can separate the sounds in the word like this: **croc** **o** **dile**

Knowing how to count the syllables in words can help you to break down the words into units to make them easier to spell.

It can also help you to remember spelling patterns.

Take this example:

★ **play ing**

If you break the word into syllables and you know how to spell **play** and the spelling pattern **-ing**, it is much easier to spell the word.

1. Can you hear how many syllables there are in the following words? Tick the correct box.

	1 SYLLABLE	2 SYLLABLES	3 SYLLABLES
develop			
lunch			
flower			
umbrella			
under			
medicine			
cold			
written			
possible			
butterfly			
hole			
lady			
baby			

These syllables are mixed up. Put them in the correct order and write out the word. The first one has been done for you.

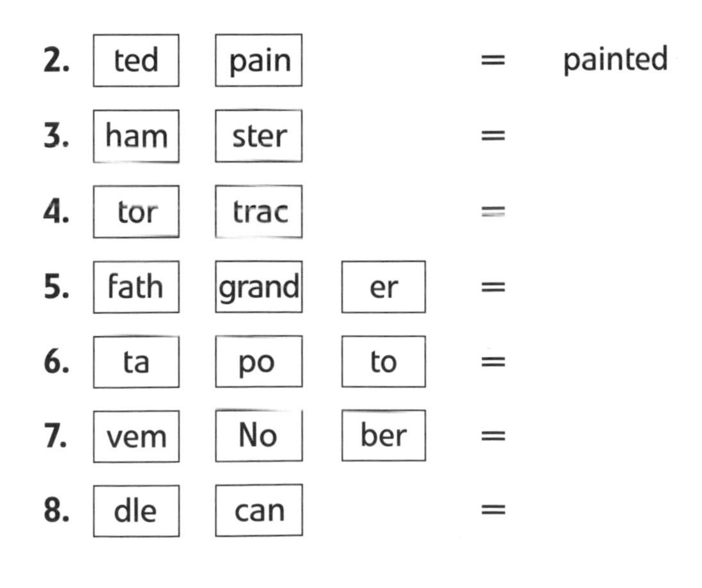

2. ted pain = painted

3. ham ster =

4. tor trac =

5. fath grand er =

6. ta po to =

7. vem No ber =

8. dle can =

Synonyms

A synonym is a word that has roughly the same meaning as another word *("syn", in Latin, means "the same").*

It is important to vary the vocabulary that we use when writing as sometimes we can get lazy and use the same words over and over. This is very boring for the reader! Lists of synonyms can be found in a book called a **thesaurus**. Take, for example, the word "big" which can often be overused when we are writing. If we want to find some other words with a similar meaning, we can go to our thesaurus and locate the word "big". Next to it will be a list of words with similar meanings, for example:

Big: large, huge, jumbo, gigantic, enormous

Here are some other examples of synonyms:

Beautiful: attractive, delightful, good-looking

Nice: fine, good, likeable

You need to be careful to make sure that the synonym you choose is right for your sentence. Sometimes a thesaurus will give you lots of alternative words but not all of them will make sense in your sentence. Look at the example below:

★ This food is **bad**.

Let's look at some alternatives:

★ This food is **disgusting**.
★ This food is **naughty**.

The first example makes sense but the second one doesn't. It is generally a good idea only to use words that you have heard before and to read the sentence to see if it sounds right.

1. Use a thesaurus to find synonyms for these words:

cold	hot	nice	like	good

2. Can you join the words from the first column to the appropriate synonym in the second?

nice	fine
big	dreadful
horrible	freezing
messy	immense
cold	untidy

Complete the sentences, using a similar word to the one in brackets.

3. My little sister has a ________________ Teddy Bear. (small)
4. Those crisps were ________________ . (tasty)
5. The garden was ________________ . (large)
6. The dog was ________________ after his swim in the sea. (wet)
7. The cat ran ________________ up the road. (quickly)

Long Vowel Sounds

ee ea ay ai y igh i_e oa oo a_e

These are all examples of **long vowel sounds.**

Read your favourite book. Can you find many words with these sounds in them?

Here are some of the most common examples:

LONG VOWEL SOUNDS:	EXAMPLES:
ee	tree, sleep, bee
ea	meat, beat, meal
ay	play, away, hay
ai	sail, wait, rain
a_e	gate, race, snake
y	cry, July, sky
igh	high, night, light
i_e	rice, nice, mice
oa	road, soak, soap
oo	root, spoon, moon

You will see that some of these sound the same but are written differently. For example, you may notice that the words **high**, **cry** and **lie** have the same vowel sound but are spelt differently.

Test 34

1. Can you fill in the gaps, using the rhyming words below?

say	way	play	day	stay

The cow was here to ___stay___ .

All he wanted was his ___________ .

He huffed and puffed as if to ___________ ,

Hurry up I've not got all ___________ .

I just want to go and ___________ .

Fill in the missing long vowel sounds in the sentences below:

igh	ay	y	ee	oa	ea

2. The d ________ was bright and sunn ________ .

3. The kite went h ________ er and h ________ er.

4. I met my friend by the corner of the str ________ t.

5. The car bumped down the dusty r ________ d.

6. P ________ p through the key hole and s ________ if they are asl ________ p.

7. M ________ cat loves to eat m ________ t.

Tick the words that contain a long vowel sound.

8. teacher ☐

9. weep ☐

10. rise ☐

11. success ☐

12. pail ☐

13. might ☐

14. bitter ☐

15. beautiful ☐

16. letter ☐

Silent Letters

Some words in English have silent letters which are not sounded in the pronunciation of the words. A long time ago, people in England did pronounce these silent letters. For example, "knife" would have been pronounced "k-nife". However, although these letters are still written today, they are no longer pronounced.

Here are a few patterns:

e final is usually silent as in – brave, crime and marble.

e is often silent before "d" as in – bribed, changed and struggled.

e is often silent before "l" as in – drivel, towel and shovel.

e is often silent before "n" as in – taken, garden and hidden.

i is sometimes silent before "l" as in – weevil and evil.

i is sometimes silent before "n" as in – basin and cousin.

k is always silent before "n" as in – knee, knew and know.

h is silent in – honest and heir.

g is silent before "m" and "n" as in – gnat and diaphragm.

d is silent in some words such as Wednesday and sometimes before "g" as in – badge.

b is silent after "m" and before "t" as in – comb, lamb, tomb and doubt.

c is sometimes silent before "k" and after "s" as in – sack, sceptre and muscle.

w is sometimes silent before "r" as in – wrong and write.

t is sometimes silent after "s" as in – fasten and listen.

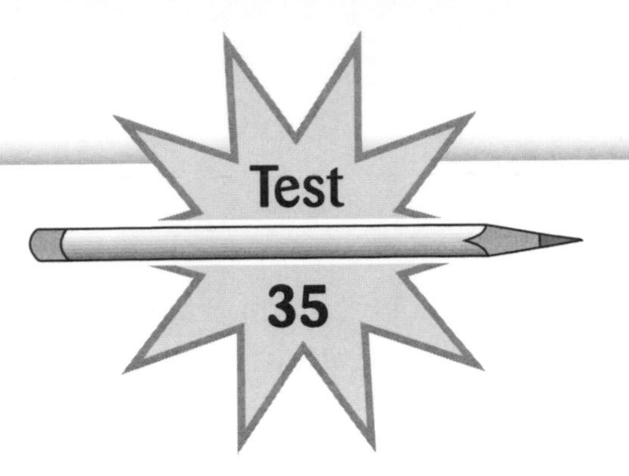

1. These words contain some letters that are silent. Can you sort them into the table?

comb, wrong, gnash, sign, reign, lamb
writing, gnome, listen, foreign, fasten, gnat
knife, knew, knowledge, wrap, thumb, design
climb, wrist, knock, knuckle, kneel, resign

SILENT B	SILENT G	SILENT K	SILENT W	SILENT T

Can you use the clues to identify words with a silent letter?

2. Granny does this to make jumpers and scarves. k___

3. Monkeys do this to get up a tree. c____

4. It is not correct. w____

5. We cut food with this. k____

6. A reply to a question. a_____

7. A tiny man figure who stands in a garden. g____

Spelling Revision

This revision section focuses on your knowledge of letters and sounds, as well as all the different spelling patterns that you have been investigating.

Alphabetical order

1. Put these letters in their alphabetical order.

g j z m p l a r s

____ ____ ____ ____ ____ ____ ____ ____ ____

Check whether these words are in alphabetical order. Tick the examples that are correct.

2. box table man people ☐

3. dog frog giraffe horse ☐

4. church house xylophone mood ☐

Check whether these words are in alphabetical order. You will need to look carefully at the second letter in each word. Tick the examples that are correct.

5. banana blue bright by ☐

6. against although angry ask ☐

7. Harry horse he how ☐

8. Match each word to its meaning. Use a dictionary to look up the words if you are not sure. The first one has been done for you.

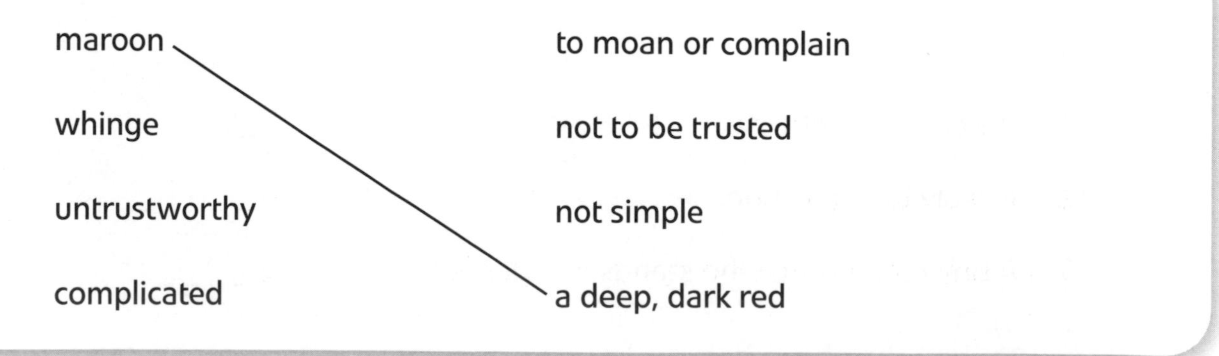

Homophones and homonyms

1. Why are "witch" and "which" homophones?

____

Which of these homophones make sense in the sentences below? Write the correct word in the space provided.

2. I couldn't help but ____________ at the man. (stare/stair)

3. I climbed up carefully one ____________ at a time. (stare/stair)

4. The ____________ ran across the park. (deer/dear)

5. That is a very ____________ price to pay. (deer/dear)

6. What is a homonym?

____

7. Why is "watch" a homonym?

____

Look up these homonyms in the dictionary. You should be able to find at least two different meanings for each word. Write two sentences for each word explaining its different meanings.

8. present

a. ____

b. ____

9. iron

a. ____

b. ____

Spelling Revision

Synonyms

Complete these sentences:

1. A synonym for large would be _______________ .

2. We use synonyms when ____________________________________

____ .

3. Draw lines to match the synonyms. The first one has been done for you. You will find that two words do not match. Find them and complete the sentence below.

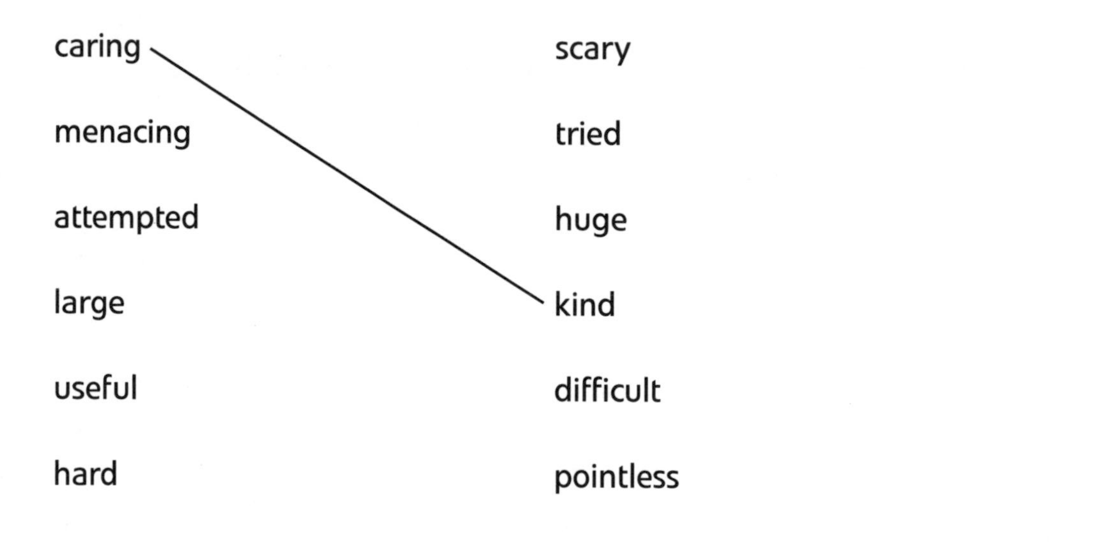

The words that are not synonyms are ___________ and ___________ .

Which synonyms are most appropriate for these sentences? Choose the word that has the most impact and delete the other word. The first one has been done for you.

4. The builders are ~~making~~/building a house.

5. Priestlys manufacture/make pizzas.

6. It is easy/cosy by the fire.

7. The hamster munched/ate his food.

8. The cat skipped/jumped on to the bed.

9. This food is nice/tasty!

10. Your birthday is a special/unusual day.

11. The giant was giant/huge.

12. I find long walks very pleasant/good.

13. The boy put/turned the light on.

14. Use a thesaurus to find synonyms for the colours: brown, purple, blue and red. Then group the colours below into the appropriate boxes.

magenta	violet	indigo	cerise
lavender	mauve	crimson	scarlet
turquoise	aquamarine	chestnut	mahogany

brown	**purple**	**blue**	**red**

Spelling Revision

Plurals

1. Which of these nouns are singular and which are plural? Group them in the correct boxes below.

granny	table	pencils	husband
countries	chairs	kitchen	mugs
bottle	taps	radiator	bulb

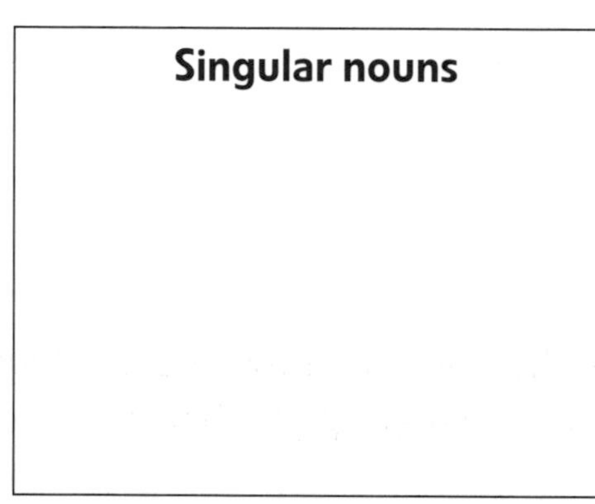

Plural nouns

Fill in the gaps with the plural form of the noun in brackets.

2. Black ________________ are delicious. (cherry)

3. Children often like to look after ________________ . (baby)

4. The ________________ were put in the cupboard. (glass)

5. ________________ grow in the summer. (strawberry)

6. Ants live in ________________ . (colony)

7. I have very strong ________________ . (belief)

8. During the summer ice ________________ cool us down. (lolly)

9. Africa contains many different ________________ . (country)

10. ________________ cross the Channel to France. (ferry)

11. ________________ hunt in packs. (wolf)

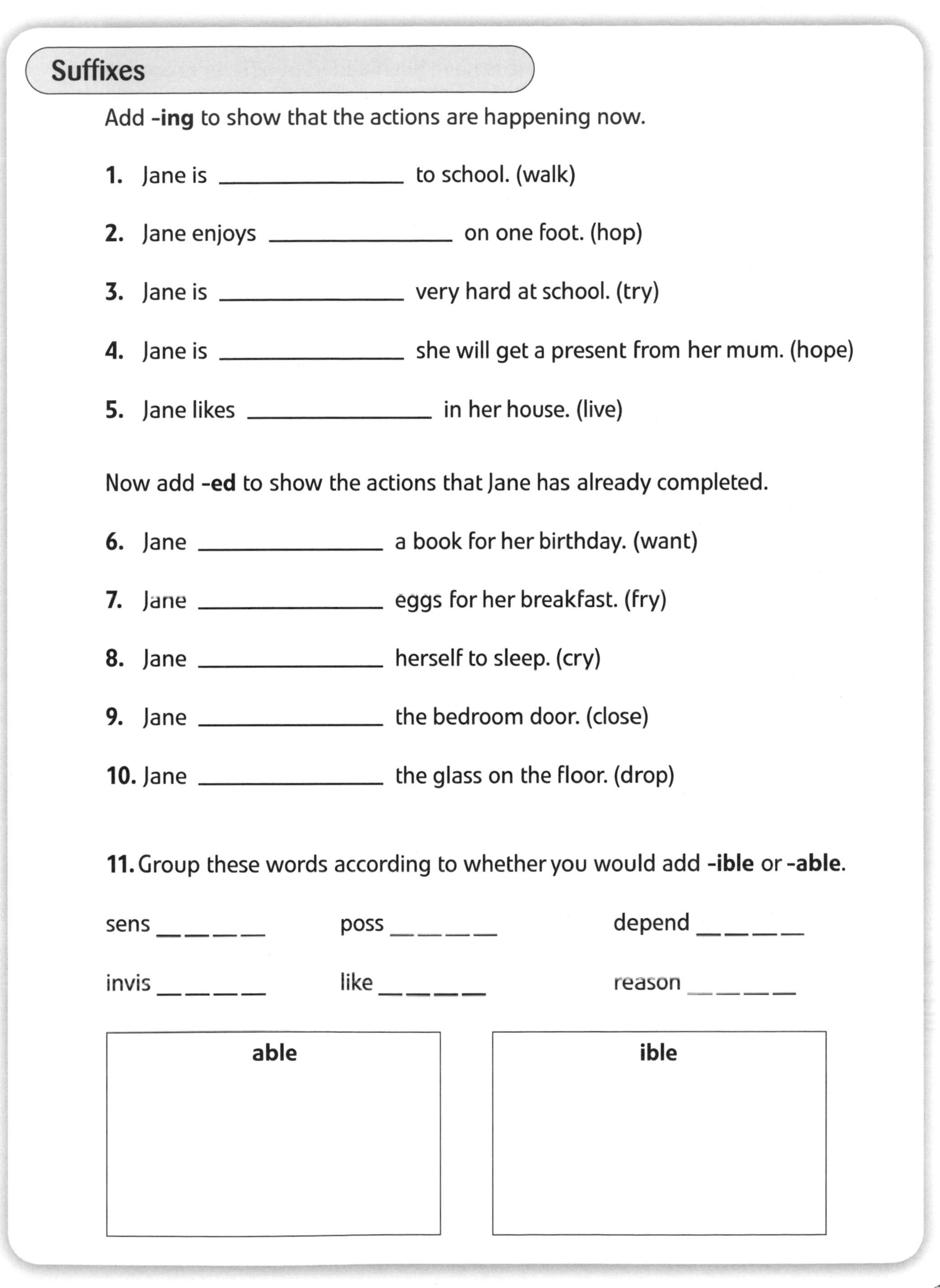

Suffixes

Add **-ing** to show that the actions are happening now.

1. Jane is ______________ to school. (walk)

2. Jane enjoys ______________ on one foot. (hop)

3. Jane is ______________ very hard at school. (try)

4. Jane is ______________ she will get a present from her mum. (hope)

5. Jane likes ______________ in her house. (live)

Now add **-ed** to show the actions that Jane has already completed.

6. Jane ______________ a book for her birthday. (want)

7. Jane ______________ eggs for her breakfast. (fry)

8. Jane ______________ herself to sleep. (cry)

9. Jane ______________ the bedroom door. (close)

10. Jane ______________ the glass on the floor. (drop)

11. Group these words according to whether you would add **-ible** or **-able**.

sens _ _ _ _ poss _ _ _ _ depend _ _ _ _

invis _ _ _ _ like _ _ _ _ reason _ _ _ _

able	**ible**

Spelling Revision

12. The suffixes **-ly**, **-ful** and **-less** have been added to different root words in the table below. In each case, identify whether the word is correct and, if it is, explain what it means. You may find a dictionary useful.

WORD	TICK/CROSS	MEANING
quickly		
careful		
quickful		
thoughtly		
faithful		
ruthless		
faithly		
rueful		
carely		
proudful		
slowless		

Check these sentences to see if the correct suffix – **-tion**, **-sion** or **-cian** – has been used. Tick the sentences if they are correct or write the correct spelling alongside.

13. The musician played beautiful music. ☐ ________________

14. I can look up definicians in the dictionary. ☐ ________________

15. That acsion was unnecessary. ☐ ________________

16. What a lovely combination! ☐ ________________

17. That is an awful situacian to be in. ☐ ________________

18. Our nasion always supports football. ☐ ________________

19. You can't trust polititions. ☐ ________________

20. We went to visit our relasions. ☐ ________________

21. I would like to get many qualifications from school. ☐ ______________

22. I refused to sign the petician. ☐ ______________

Which of these adjectives are superlatives and which are comparatives? Write "superlative" or "comparative" next to the words below.

23. biggest ______________

24. stronger ______________

25. heavier ______________

26. smallest ______________

27. trendiest ______________

28. darker ______________

29. thinnest ______________

30. happier ______________

31. drier ______________

32. saddest ______________

Now write a sentence using each of the words above to show their meaning.

33. ____

____

34. ____

____

35. ____

____

Spelling Revision

36. ______________________________

____

37. ______________________________

____

38. ______________________________

____

39. ______________________________

____

40. ______________________________

____

41. ______________________________

____

42. ______________________________

____

Complete these sentences so that they make sense:

43. This bedroom is ______________ than the other one. (larger/largest)

44. I am the ______________ person in the world! (happier/happiest)

45. You are ______________ than me. (shorter/shortest)

46. I am the ______________ child in my class. (lighter/lightest)

47. This is the ______________ day of the year. (longer/longest)

Prefixes

Write at least two examples of words that have the following prefixes. You can use a dictionary to help you.

1. re ____________ ____________

2. mis ____________ ____________

3. non ____________ ____________

4. dis ____________ ____________

5. un ____________ ____________

6. Some prefixes have similar meanings and we can use the wrong one by mistake. Check these words and tick those that have the correct prefix.

MEANING	WORD	CORRECT OR INCORRECT?
not even	diseven	
not healthy	dishealthy	
not loyal	unloyal	
invent again	reinvent	
opposite of wrap	unwrap	
work together	cooperate	
not understood	misunderstood	
not making sense	dissense	
not liking	nonlike	
look again	review	

Spelling Revision

Syllables

How many syllables do each of these words have?

1. many ☐
2. two ☐
3. hitting ☐
4. compliment ☐
5. football ☐
6. washing ☐
7. hospital ☐
8. naughty ☐
9. child ☐
10. children ☐

11. Now think of your own words with differing numbers of syllables. Complete the table below.

1 SYLLABLE	2 SYLLABLES	3 SYLLABLES	4 SYLLABLES

Long vowel sounds

Read these words and underline the letters that represent the long vowel sound. The first one has been done for you.

1. s<u>igh</u>
2. sail
3. three
4. say
5. moat
6. hoot
7. mate
8. beat
9. late
10. dry

11. Complete this table by giving at least two examples of each of the long vowel sounds representing a long "a".

Long vowel sound	Examples of words containing that spelling
a	
ay	
ai	
a_e	
eigh	

Circle the word that has the correct long vowel sound.

12. lie/ligh

13. trie/try

14. whie/why

15. sigh/sie

16. my/mie

Spelling Revision

Silent letters

Write an example of a word that contains a:

1. silent w ______________________
2. silent k ______________________
3. silent e ______________________
4. silent g ______________________
5. silent t ______________________
6. silent c ______________________
7. silent b ______________________
8. silent d ______________________

Underline the silent letters in these words. Sshhh!

9. tomb
10. mitten
11. wreck
12. gnome
13. climb
14. science
15. knife
16. hedge
17. hour
18. knack

Now write a sentence for each word.

19. ____

20. ____

21. ______________________________

22. ______________________________

23. ______________________________

24. ______________________________

25. ______________________________

26. ______________________________

27. ______________________________

28. ______________________________

Use the clues to identify words with a silent letter and fill in the gaps.

29. A baby cat is called this. k _ _ _ _ _

30. The day that follows Tuesday. W _ _ _ _ _ _ _ _

31. A synonym for truthful. h _ _ _ _ _

32. Part of your leg. k _ _ _

33. Used to brush your hair. c _ _ _

34. You learn to read and … w _ _ _ _

35. Used to keep a door open. w _ _ _ _

36. A jumper can be this. k _ _ _ _ _ _

37. Somebody who ascends cliffs. c _ _ _ _ _ _

Answers

Test 1
1. ✓
2. -
3. ✓
4. -
5. -
6. ✓
7. ✓
8. ✓
9. -
10. ✓
11. At last, the postman came.
12. The car had been stolen.
13. I had fish and chips for tea.
14. Adam wanted a football.
15. How did you mend the fence?
16. I have won the lottery!
17. When did you arrive?
18. It was cold at the seaside.
19. Stanley began to sing.
20. Where shall I meet you?

Test 2
1. bird
2. boy
3. mouse
4. paint
5. man
6. girl, school
7. teacher, report
8. woman, room
9. boy, fish, cup, bridge, river, book, clock, rabbit, dress, toffee, bedroom
10. popstar
11. book
12. jelly, cake

Test 3
1–5.

Proper nouns:
Beckham, Manchester United, October, Friday, Sunday, Queen Elizabeth II, Paris, Channel Tunnel

Common nouns:
football, birthday, days, bridge, class

6. pack
7. flock
8. shoal
9. class
10. swarm
11. flock

Test 4
1. Abstract nouns:

justice, love, envy, faith, resentment, truth, jealousy, fear, hate, hope

Common nouns:

2. armchair, arm + chair
3. postman, post + man
4. teapot, tea + pot
5. toothbrush, tooth + brush
6. playpen, play + pen

Test 5
1. Any suitable examples.
2. The boy stared at the monster. The monster stared back at the boy. Suddenly, the boy turned and ran as fast as **he** could. Screeching at the top of **its** voice, the monster gave chase. Closer and closer **it** came until, with a mighty leap, **it** seized the boy. The boy gave a loud scream and the monster dropped **him**. The boy ran home to **his** mother. **She** cuddled **him** and then **she** phoned the police.

Test 6
1. cooks
2. walked
3. am writing

4. will run
5. waited
6. was drinking
7. buys
8. loves
9. wants
10. am telephoning
11. read
12. rides
13. cries
14. laughs
15. writes

Test 7

1. skips, present
2. wanted, past
3. will enter, future
4. passed, past
5. love, present
6. am, present
7. will chew, future
8. polished, past
9. will enjoy, future
10. had
11. will
12. will
13. were
14. will
15. had
16. is

Test 8

1. crack
2. add
3. sprinkle
4. whisk
5. heat
6. pour
7. cook
8. turn
9. serve
10. Next week, there will be a fete at the school. There will be many stalls. The cake stall will be popular and will sell a wide range of cakes and sweets. The raffle will/should raise at least £200 for the school. The fete will be opened by the mayor, and she will give a donation to the school on behalf of the council. The fete will begin at 2 o'clock and will finish at 4 o'clock. The school will be delighted if enough money is raised to buy four new computers.

Test 9

1. and
2. or
3. but
4. and
5. or
6. I liked the flowers and the animals.
7. Mum bought a cake and biscuits.
8. Shall I turn left or right?
9. -
10. I enjoy television and tennis.
11. -

Test 10

1. April was excited, because she had won the raffle.
2. Although it was a sunny day, Bill wore his coat.
3. Robyn, laughing softly, crept out of the room.
4. Because he dropped his ice cream, Jake cried.
5. The dog, wagging its tail, ran towards the cat.
6. After spitting at the dog, the cat turned and jumped on to the fence.
7. when/before
8. because
9. before
10. although
11. because
12. so
13. before
14. so

Test 11

1. hot
2. fierce
3. strong
4. grey
5. miserable
6. funny
7. small
8. delicious
9. beautiful
10. happy
11. furious
12. wise
13. bold
14. boastful
15. tiny
16. mean

Answers

Test 12

1. **BRAVE:**

COWARDLY:

HAPPY:

SAD:

Test 13

1. these
2. her
3. every
4. their
5. our, your
6. my, that
7. this, our
8. each
9. those
10. that, this
11. his
12. their
13. my
14. your
15. our
16. its
17. your
18. their
19. her
20. my

Test 14

1. stroked, lovingly
2. ran, quickly
3. walked, unsteadily
4. moved, gracefully
5. painted, beautifully
6. Alice stopped abruptly and listened carefully. She could hear a groaning sound coming from the house. She walked slowly up the narrow garden path, stopping occasionally to listen for the noise. She hammered loudly on the door, but there was no answer. She took a deep breath and pushed firmly. The door swung open. She went in. With each step she took, the floorboards creaked loudly. Then the door of the bathroom opened and her father came out singing. The groaning noise was her father's awful singing!
7-10. Any suitable adverbs.

GRAMMAR REVISION
Sentences
1-10.

Sentences
2, 3, 6, 8, 10

Not sentences
1, 4, 5, 7, 9

11. simple
12. compound
13. simple
14. compound
15. compound
16. and, but, or
17. Whatever the weather, I enjoy walking.
18. Although the news is normally on late at night, I always stay up to watch it.
19. The girl couldn't go to school because she felt so unwell.
20. After trying so hard, Paul was disappointed that he didn't win the race.
21. Karen, chuckling softly to herself, hid under the blanket.

Answers

22. The man, who had been watching TV for a while, had fallen asleep.

23.

Main clauses	Subordinate clauses
I felt tired	because it is more interesting than classical music.
It was raining outside	so I went to bed early.
I enjoy pop music	before she spoke to the teacher.
Janet thought about it carefully	so I decided not to go out.
The postman was late	although I quite like purple too.
Pink is my favourite colour	which got him into trouble.

Nouns

1. ✓
2. -
3. ✓
4. ✓
5. ✓
6. ✓
7. -
8. ✓
9. -
10. ✓
11. ✓
12. ✓
13. -
14. -
15. ✓
16. -
17. A proper noun is the name of a particular or special person or thing, e.g. France, Peter.
18. A proper noun begins with a capital letter.
19. Charlie (circled), clown, trousers, nose (underlined)
20. Medway, Rochester (circled), river (underlined)
21. oranges, apples, fruit (underlined)
22. Caroline (circled), teacher (underlined)
23. sister, birthday (underlined), June (circled)
24. Paris, France
25. George
26. Tuesday
27. Harry Potter
28. Tower of London
29. pack
30. gaggle
31. audience
32. flight
33. family
34.

bookworm, bookcase, houseboat, housekeeper, housewife, boathouse, goalkeeper, casebook

Pronouns

1. he
2. it
3. they
4. she
5. yours
6. yours, mine
7. its
8. theirs

Verbs

1. walk
2. slept
3. wanted, visit
4. am going
5. were thinking
6. stopped
7. went
8. drove
9. came, was clawing
10. tell
11. enjoyed
12. played
13. polished
14. asked
15. went
16.

Present go, is, has, make, are

Past had, wanted, were, talked, went, was, did, made

Future will have, will be

17. Any suitable answers.
18. During the Victorian era children were employed to do a variety of unpleasant jobs. One of the worst jobs was working in a cotton mill. The children had to work incredibly hard. They crawled under heavy machinery and risked their lives every day. In addition, they were not paid very much and lived in cramped,

Answers

squalid conditions. Most children who worked in cotton mills were orphans, so they did not even have a family's love and support. Do you think you would have enjoyed working in a cotton mill?

19. The text should be written in the past tense because the events discussed have already happened.

20. Instructions are written in the present tense because you complete the actions step by step.

21. We use the future tense when we talk about something that will happen in the future.

Adverbs

1. slowly
2. carefully
3. gently
4. fiercely
5. cheerfully
6. furiously
7. quickly
8. ruthlessly
9. fantastically
10. grumpily
11. occasionally
12. rarely
13. usually
14. now
15. soon

16. Jane stood outside Becky's house and wondered if her friend would answer the door. She was sure that Becky was inside because she could hear music coming from the lounge. She was probably gazing dreamily at her David Beckham poster, Jane concluded. This often happened. Just as she was about to give up and go home, she caught sight of a figure tramping downstairs. "Sometimes," thought Jane, "you make me so cross!"

17-18. Any suitable answers.

Adjectives

1. crazy
2. pretty
3. tired
4. sandy
5. sad
6-10. Any suitable answers
11. The child, who was clever, learnt his spellings.
12. The black and white cat was mewing loudly.
13. The child, who was angry, stamped his feet.
14. The youngest member of the class was Charlie.

15.

generous	grumpy
noisy	kind
moody	ebony
tired	loud
black	fatigued
royal	fair
just	princely

Determiners

1. her
2. their
3. every
4. that
5. my
6. your
7. these
8. our
9. the
10. each

Grammar summary

Adverbs
happily
hesitantly

Pronouns
we

Determiners
his

Nouns
batsman
fruit

Answers

Verbs
was
scored
played
is
rose

Adjectives
good

Test 15

1. full stop
2. apostrophe
3. question mark
4. speech marks
5. comma
6. exclamation mark
7. The sun is shining.
8. Oranges are juicy.
9. Shall we go to the cinema?
10. This is ridiculous!
11. How are you?
12. I will go shopping with Amy and Ian.
13. We will take our holiday in June.
14. Sarah will be arriving on Monday.
15. Do you live in London?
16. Adam wants to meet the Queen.

Test 16

1. Peter wanted a bike. He wanted to buy the one in the shop. He didn't have enough money. He decided to ask his dad. His dad told him he could buy it on his birthday.

2. Sally looked for her cat. She couldn't find it anywhere. Suddenly she saw the tip of a ginger tail behind a plant pot. She crept up to the pot. It wasn't her cat. It was a kitten. Then she saw a pair of ears sticking out from under the table. It was her cat, Ginger.

Test 17

1.

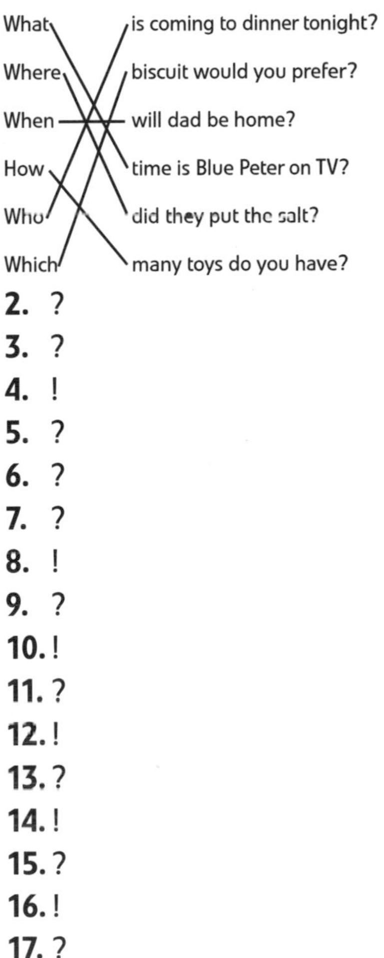

2. ?
3. ?
4. !
5. ?
6. ?
7. ?
8. !
9. ?
10. !
11. ?
12. !
13. ?
14. !
15. ?
16. !
17. ?

Test 18

1. I need to buy bananas, crisps, apples, milk, butter, eggs and ham.
2. Beckham, Giggs, Scholes, Butt and Neville are my favourite players.
3. For the school play we would like white shirts, black plimsolls, blue trousers and a red scarf.
4. Pupils should bring pencils, pens, a ruler, a rubber, a pencil sharpener and a pair of compasses.
5. In my suitcase I must put sunglasses, underwear, a towel, toothpaste and a toothbrush.
6. I went home, ate my tea, had a bath and watched television.
7. Sally, our mum, is a teacher.
8. I met Billy, your brother, at the pool.
9. Although I was tired, I stayed up late.
10. Blake, the head boy, spoke at assembly.
11. Putting on her socks, Sarah sang a tune.
12. Alex, a toddler, cheered the clown.
13. If you don't hurry, we'll be late.

Answers

Test 19

1. the skin of the rabbit
2. the book of Mary
3. the bark of the dog
4. the voice of John
5. the success of the footballer
6. boy's
7. Saturday's
8. bride's
9. sister's
10. Dad's
11. plural
12. possessive
13. possessive
14. possessive
15. plural

Test 20

1a. singular
1b. plural
2a. plural
2b. singular
3a. singular
3b. plural
4a. singular
4b. plural
5. James'/James's hat
6. Francis'/Francis's hair
7. Charles'/Charles's car
8. the women's skirts
9. the dogs' tails
10. -
11. ✓
12. ✓
13. -

Test 21

1. I will
2. she had or would
3. will not
4. you will
5. he is or has
6. I am
7. I'd
8. I'm
9. it's
10. you've
11. don't
12. isn't
13. they're
14. I've
15. I've
16. don't
17. won't
18. it's
19. they're
20. don't

Test 22

1. Robert asked, "Is it time for tea?"
2. Ben muttered, "It's not fair."
3. "I need some new shoes," said the old lady.
4. "Can you direct me to the hospital?" asked the driver.
5. "I wish I hadn't come," moaned Fiona. "I should have stayed in bed."
6. "Who would like a balloon?" asked the clown.
7. "He made a rabbit disappear!" gasped Annie.

PUNCTUATION REVISION

Punctuating a sentence

1. Cats can be fluffy and soft.
2. Sometimes we enjoy doing our homework.
3. School ends at three o'clock.
4. Stop doing that!
5. My favourite lesson is English.
6. My sister's name is Cathy.
7. Why is John crying?
8. Her birthday is in December.
9. I like cake and I like biscuits.

Answers

10.

You use capital letters for…	An example is…
Proper nouns – names of people/places	Jimmy, London
At the start of a sentence	Do you like me?

11. Goldilocks lowered herself on to the chair and boy did she get a shock. The chair collapsed underneath her leaving her sprawling on the floor. However, she was not to be beaten and so she climbed the creaky stairs to the top of the house. What she found were three different sized rooms, each with their own bed. "Excellent," she thought to herself. "Now I can get a proper rest."
12. ?
13. .
14. !
15. .
16. ?
17. ?
18. .
29. !
20. !
21. ?
22. We use a question mark at the end of a question.
23. We use an exclamation mark to add emphasis to what has been said, e.g. to show surprise or anger.
24. When do you/we have assembly?
25. When do you/we play football?
26. Who did you make your musical instrument with?
27. Do you enjoy coming to school?
28. How many centimetres are in a metre?
29. what
30. who
31. where
32. which
33. when
34. ✓
35. My sister is ugly, annoying and rude.
36. We plan to travel to Africa, America, New Zealand and Australia.
37. The shopping list included milk, bread and cheese.
38. The naughty girl, Goldilocks, knocked on the door.
39. Greedily, she ate the porridge.
40. Climbing up the stairs, Goldilocks sighed to herself.

Apostrophes

1-5. Any suitable answers.
6.

Word	Contracted version
do not	don't
let us	let's
did not	didn't
I am	I'm
can not	can't

7. It's not raining now.
8. We'll be late if we don't hurry.
9. Linda won't tell us what she's making.
10. We're sure she saw us.
11. I'm feeling tired today.
12. its
13. it's
14. it's
15. it's
16. its

Answers

17.

Possessive words	Words in their longer form
Jenny's pencil	the pencil of Jenny
the cat's whiskers	the whiskers of the cat
Susan's bag	the bag of Susan
the man's beard	the beard of the man
Paul's umbrella	the umbrella of Paul
the teacher's glasses	the glasses of the teacher
the woman's brush	the brush of the woman
the frog's legs	the legs of the frog
Mary's cake	the cake of Mary
the boy's sweets	the sweets of the boy

18. singular
19. singular
20. plural
21. singular
22. plural

Speech marks
1. "Give that to me," said John.
2. "I don't know," replied the boy.
3. "Who would like a cup of tea?" the secretary asked.
4. Steven whispered, "What did you say?"
5. Jamie gasped, "Oh no not again!"
6. "Oh no," moaned Peter, "you'll never guess what I've done."
7. "Come inside at once," said Dad. "You're late as it is."
8. "Please mum," said Mark, "can I go to Stephen's house?"
9. "Yes, I did eat all the cake," admitted Andrew, "but I was very hungry."
10. "Have you seen my dog?" the old man inquired. "It ran off early this morning."

Punctuation summary
1. "Listen to me class. I have something interesting to tell you," began Miss Black. "We are going on a trip next Tuesday to the Roman villa."
"Excellent," chorused the class. They listened carefully as Miss Black explained the kinds of activities they would be doing. She told them about the Roman artefacts they would see, the tour of the villa and the treasure hunt they would enjoy after lunch.
"Can we bring our own packed lunch?" asked Paul.
"I'm going to have a wagon wheel!" exclaimed one girl.
"You can bring whatever you like – it's totally up to you," concluded Miss Black.

Test 23
1. ant, dog, elephant, lion, zebra
2. boy, child, girl, lady, man
3. flower, grow, hat, pond, seed
4. cabbage, cheese, cider, corn, crisps
5. sand, sea, spade, starfish, sun
6. off, olive, on, out, oven
7-11. Any appropriate definitions.

Test 24
1. two
2. sail
3. hour
4. bare
5. heel
6. plane
7. hear
8. hair
9-13. Any suitable sentences. For example:
9a. A business that looks after people's money.
b. The raised ground along the edge of a river or lake.
10a. A message written on paper and sent to someone.
b. One of the written symbols that go together to make words.

Answers

11a. A small circle of metal that you wear on your finger.
b. If you ring someone, you phone them.
12a. A competition to see who is fastest at something.
b. A large group of people who look alike in some way.
13a. A small clock, usually worn on a strap on a person's wrist.
b. If you watch something, you look at it for some time and pay attention to what is happening.

Test 25

1.

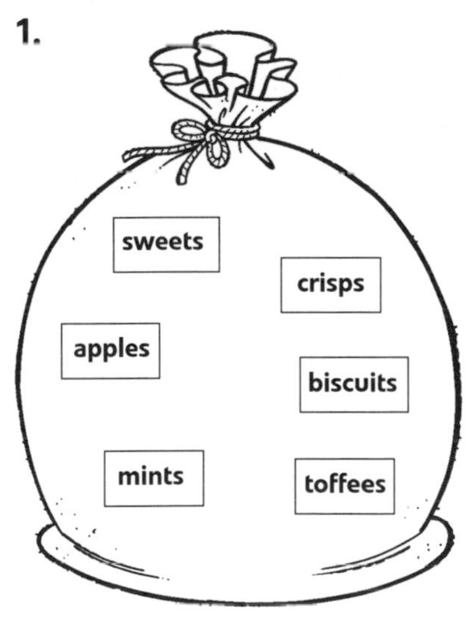

2. ladies
3. wolves
4. boxes
5. flies
6. children
7. knives
8. witches
9. fish

Test 26

1. having
2. looking
3. swimming
4. putting
5. hopping
6. chatting
7. chopping
8-9. Any suitable verbs ending in –ing.
10. weighed
creamed
stirred
poured
cooked
tried

Test 27

1. possible
2. suitable
3. sensible
4. invisible
5. fashionable
6. comfortable
7. terrible
8. enjoyable
9. possible/sensible/comfortable/enjoyable
10. fashionable/suitable/comfortable
11. sensible
12. terrible
13. suitable
14. invisible
15. comfortable
16. enjoyable
17. possible

Test 28

1.

	COMPARATIVES	**SUPERLATIVES**
light	lighter	lightest
tall	taller	tallest
full	fuller	fullest
dark	darker	darkest
soft	softer	softest
old	older	oldest
slow	slower	slowest
fast	faster	fastest
high	higher	highest
low	lower	lowest
fat	fatter	fattest
thin	thinner	thinnest
cold	colder	coldest
hot	hotter	hottest
sad	sadder	saddest
wide	wider	widest
happy	happier	happiest
dry	drier	driest

Answers

2. hottest
3. shiniest
4. bigger
5. tastiest

Test 29

1. liberation
2. position
3. musician
4. information
5. nation
6. combination
7. diversion
8. mathematician
9. situation
10. petition
11. politician
12. quotation
13. education
14. qualification
15. magician
16. occupation
17. punctuation
18. association
19. exclamation
20. deprivation
21. competition
22. population
23. electrician
24. imagination

Test 30

1. thoughtful, thoughtless
2. useful, useless
3. sadly
4. bashful
5. kindly

Test 31

1. uneven
2. dishonest
3. unhealthy
4. unwrap
5. disobey
6. unfortunate
7. unknown
8. distrust
9. disapprove
10. unfair
11.

mis
misunderstood
misread

re
reread
redesign
rewrite
refuse

non
non-fiction
non-stop

un
uncertain
unusual

mini
miniskirt

de
defuse

Test 32

1.

	1 SYLLABLE	2 SYLLABLES	3 SYLLABLES
develop			✓
lunch	✓		
flower		✓	
umbrella			✓
under		✓	
medicine			✓
cold	✓		
written		✓	
possible			✓
butterfly			✓
hole	✓		
lady		✓	
baby		✓	

2. painted
3. hamster
4. tractor
5. grandfather
6. potato
7. November
8. candle

Test 33

1. Any suitable synonyms.
2.

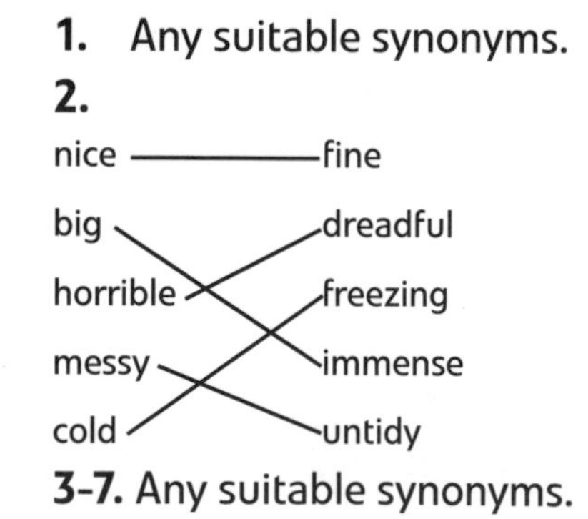

3-7. Any suitable synonyms.

Test 34

1. The cow was here to stay.
All he wanted was his way.
He huffed and puffed as if to say,
Hurry up, I've not got all day.

I just want to go and play.
2. day, sunny
3. higher, higher
4. street
5. road
6. peep, see, asleep
7. my, meat
8. ✓
9. ✓
10. ✓
11. -
12. ✓
13. ✓
14. -
15. ✓
16. -

Test 35

1.

SILENT B	SILENT G
comb climb thumb lamb	gnome gnash sign foreign reign gnat design resign

SILENT K	SILENT W
knife knew knowledge knock knuckle kneel	writing wrong wrist wrap

SILENT T
listen fasten

2. knit
3. climb
4. wrong
5. knife
6. answer
7. gnome

SPELLING REVISION

Alphabetical order

1. a, g, j, l, m, p, r, s, z
2. -
3. ✓
4. -
5. ✓
6. ✓
7. -
8. -

maroon — to moan or complain
whinge — not to be trusted
untrustworthy — not simple
complicated — a deep, dark red

Homophones and homonyms

1. "Witch" and "which" sound the same but have different meanings and different spellings.
2. stare
3. stair
4. deer
5. dear
6. A homonym is a word that has one sound and one way of being spelt but has more than one meaning.
7. "Watch" has two meanings – to observe and an object that tells the time.
8. present
a. a gift
b. the verb to give
9. iron
a. a metal
b. an object used to iron clothes

Synonyms

1. A synonym for large would be huge/giant etc.
2. We use synonyms when we want to vary our language/use an alternative word.
3.

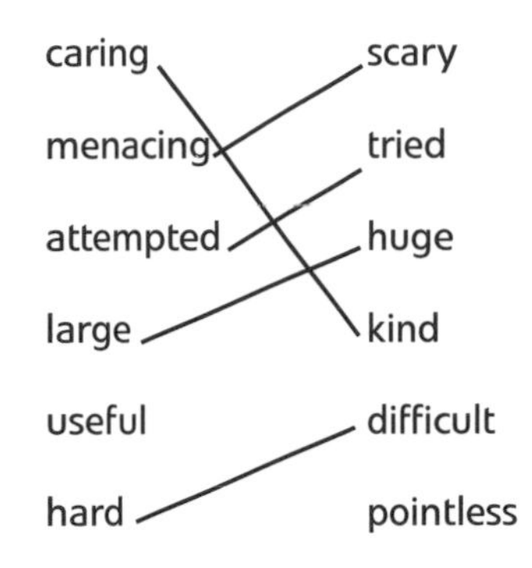

The words that are not synonyms are useful and pointless.

4. The builders are building a house.
5. Priestlys make pizzas.
6. It is cosy by the fire.
7. The hamster munched his food.
8. The cat jumped on to the bed.
9. This food is tasty!
10. Your birthday is a special day.
11. The giant was huge.
12. I find long walks very pleasant.
13. The boy turned the light on.

Answers

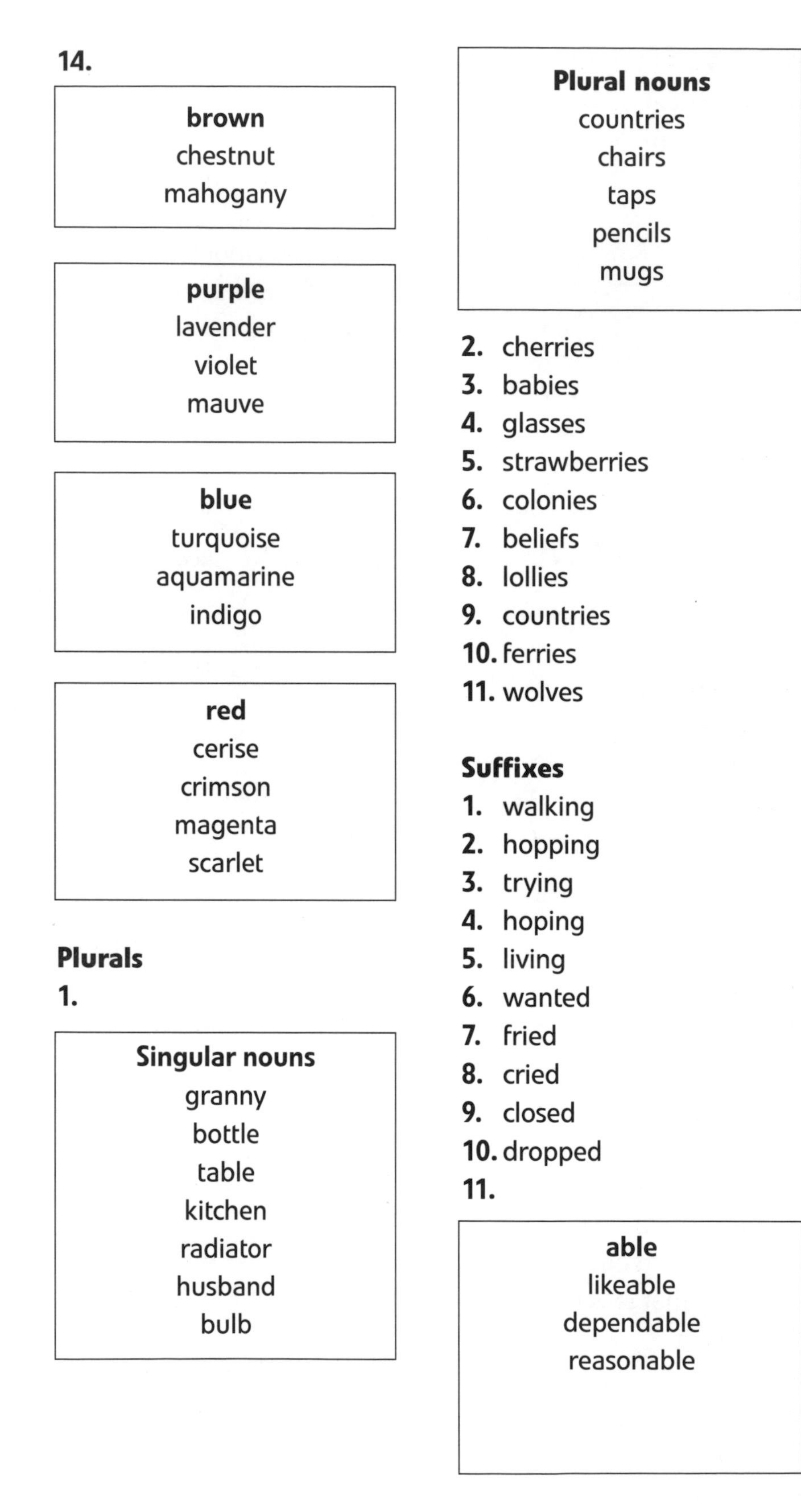

14.

brown
chestnut
mahogany

purple
lavender
violet
mauve

blue
turquoise
aquamarine
indigo

red
cerise
crimson
magenta
scarlet

Plurals

1.

Singular nouns
granny
bottle
table
kitchen
radiator
husband
bulb

Plural nouns
countries
chairs
taps
pencils
mugs

2. cherries
3. babies
4. glasses
5. strawberries
6. colonies
7. beliefs
8. lollies
9. countries
10. ferries
11. wolves

Suffixes

1. walking
2. hopping
3. trying
4. hoping
5. living
6. wanted
7. fried
8. cried
9. closed
10. dropped
11.

able
likeable
dependable
reasonable

ible
sensible
invisible
possible

12. See opposite page
13. ✓
14. definitions
15. action
16. ✓
17. situation
18. nation
19. politicians
20. relations
21. ✓
22. petition
23. superlative
24. comparative
25. comparative
26. superlative
27. superlative
28. comparative
29. superlative
30. comparative
31. comparative
32. superlative
33-42. Any suitable sentences.
43 larger
44. happiest
15. shorter
46. lightest
47. longest

Answers

12.

WORD	TICK/CROSS	MEANING
quickly	✓	fast
careful	✓	with care
quickful	✕	
thoughtly	✕	
faithful	✓	trustworthy/reliable
ruthless	✓	having no pity
faithly	✕	
rueful	✓	sad
carely	✕	
proudful	✕	
slowless	✕	

Prefixes

1-5. Any suitable answers.

6.

MEANING	WORD	CORRECT OR INCORRECT?
not even	diseven	✕ – uneven
not healthy	dishealthy	✕ – unhealthy
not loyal	unloyal	✕ – disloyal
invent again	reinvent	✓
opposite of wrap	unwrap	✓
work together	cooperate	✓
not understood	misunderstood	✓
not making sense	dissense	✕ – nonsense
not liking	nonlike	✕ – dislike
look again	review	✓

Syllables

1. 2
2. 1
3. 2
4. 3
5. 2
6. 2
7. 3
8. 2
9. 1
10. 2
11. Any suitable examples.

Long vowel sounds

1. sigh
2. sail
3. three
4. say
5. moat
6. hoot
7. mate
8. beat
9. late
10. dry

11.

Long vowel sound	Examples of words containing that spelling
a	station, nation
ay	lay, tray, may
ai	pain, train, pail
a-e	mane, lane, hate, date
eigh	neigh, weigh, eight

12. lie
13. try
14. why
15. sigh
16. my

Silent letters

1-8. Any suitable examples.
9. tomb
10. mitten
11. wreck
12. gnome
13. climb
14. science
15. knife
16. hedge
17. hour
18. knack
19-28. Any suitable examples.
29. kitten
30. Wednesday
31. honest
32. knee
33. comb
34. write
35. wedge
36. knitted
37. climber